Communications in Computer and Information Science 2831

Series Editors

Rationale

The CCIS series is devoted to the publication of proceedings of computer science conferences. Its aim is to efficiently disseminate original research results in informatics in printed and electronic form. While the focus is on publication of peer-reviewed full papers presenting mature work, inclusion of reviewed short papers reporting on work in progress is welcome, too. Besides globally relevant meetings with internationally representative program committees guaranteeing a strict peer-reviewing and paper selection process, conferences run by societies or of high regional or national relevance are also considered for publication.

Topics

The topical scope of CCIS spans the entire spectrum of informatics ranging from foundational topics in the theory of computing to information and communications science and technology and a broad variety of interdisciplinary application fields.

Information for Volume Editors and Authors

Publication in CCIS is free of charge. No royalties are paid, however, we offer registered conference participants temporary free access to the online version of the conference proceedings on SpringerLink (http://link.springer.com) by means of an http referrer from the conference website and/or a number of complimentary printed copies, as specified in the official acceptance email of the event.

CCIS proceedings can be published in time for distribution at conferences or as post-proceedings, and delivered in the form of printed books and/or electronically as USBs and/or e-content licenses for accessing proceedings at SpringerLink. Furthermore, CCIS proceedings are included in the CCIS electronic book series hosted in the SpringerLink digital library at https://link.springer.com/bookseries/7899. Conferences publishing in CCIS are allowed to use our online conference service (Meteor) for managing the whole proceedings lifecycle (from submission and reviewing to preparing for publication) free of charge.

Publication process

The language of publication is exclusively English. Authors publishing in CCIS have to sign the Springer CCIS copyright transfer form, however, they are free to use their material published in CCIS for substantially changed, more elaborate subsequent publications elsewhere. For the preparation of the camera-ready papers/files, authors have to strictly adhere to the Springer CCIS Authors' Instructions and are strongly encouraged to use the CCIS LaTeX style files or templates.

Abstracting/Indexing

CCIS is abstracted/indexed in DBLP, Google Scholar, EI-Compendex, Mathematical Reviews, SCImago, Scopus. CCIS volumes are also submitted for the inclusion in ISI Proceedings.

How to start

To start the evaluation of your proposal for inclusion in the CCIS series, please send an e-mail to ccis@springer.com

Jörg Schäfer · Juan Boubeta-Puig
Editors

Applied Computer Science

11th Spanish German Symposium, SGSOACS 2025
Vienna, Austria, June 30–July 3, 2025
Proceedings

Editors
Jörg Schäfer
Frankfurt University of Applied Sciences
Frankfurt am Main, Germany

Juan Boubeta-Puig
University of Cádiz
Cádiz, Spain

ISSN 1865-0929 ISSN 1865-0937 (electronic)
Communications in Computer and Information Science
ISBN 978-3-032-14815-5 ISBN 978-3-032-14816-2 (eBook)
https://doi.org/10.1007/978-3-032-14816-2

This Springer imprint is published by the registered company Springer Nature Switzerland AG
The registered company address is: Gewerbestrasse 11, 6330 Cham, Switzerland

Preface

This is how it all began. In 2014, two researchers from Universidad de Cádiz, Inmaculada Medina-Bulo and Francisco Palomo-Lozano, together with a friend from Frankfurt University of Applied Sciences, Martin Kappes—another friend, Matthias F. Wagner, joined them soon after—created the idea of a symposium to be held annually to foster collaboration in Applied Computer Science between Spanish and German universities—the Spanish German Symposium on Applied Computer Science SGSOACS was born! The symposium language has been the lingua franca of science today, English, and the different editions have been organized jointly by the University of Cádiz, Frankfurt University of Applied Sciences, the Complutense University of Madrid, and, recently, TU Graz. With the exception of the pandemic years 2020 and 2021, the SGSOACS have been conducted as intense in-person events at scenic venues in the host countries, promoting vibrant academic exchange in inspiring settings: 2014, Cádiz, Spain; 2015, Frankfurt, Germany; 2016, Cádiz, Spain; 2017, Frankfurt, Germany; 2018, Madrid, Spain; 2019, Frankfurt, Germany; 2020/21, online; 2022, Toledo, Spain; 2023, Tutzing, Germany; 2024, Cádiz, Spain; 2025, Vienna, Austria.

The symposium was established with the intention of providing a platform for the presentation of early-stage and speculative—sometimes highly speculative—research, encouraging open discussions and critical feedback. It primarily targets doctoral candidates and postdoctoral researchers, offering them an opportunity to receive early input on their work, while maintaining rigorous academic standards. Consequently, the SGSOACS has always required the submission of high-quality short or extended papers, each subject to a formal peer-review process prior to acceptance for presentation. Over the years, the symposium has covered a broad spectrum of topics, including but not limited to: Ambient-assisted living; artificial intelligence and machine learning; blockchain; complex event processing; computer networks; cybersecurity; data science; human-activity recognition; security; smart cities; software architectures and engineering; and software testing. Students, researchers, or professionals interested in these topics—not necessarily only from the supporting universities—have been invited to join us and participate in the event. Each edition has fostered new collaborations within the Spanish-German research community, leading to joint research efforts and scholarly publications.

Initially, symposium papers were distributed as preprints. In 2024, the contributions were published as open-access papers on Zenodo, a general-purpose repository developed under the European OpenAIRE program and operated by CERN.

The 2025 edition of SGSOACS marked two significant milestones. First, it was hosted for the first time in the beautiful city of Vienna in collaboration with the research group of FranzWotawa from Graz University of Technology. Secondly, and most notably, for the first time, the proceedings were published by Springer in the Communications in Computer and Information Science (CCIS) series—a major achievement in the history of the symposium. We extend our sincere gratitude to Springer for their excellent support and the opportunity to disseminate the contributions more broadly. All submissions underwent a rigorous single blind peer review process with each paper receiving at least three independent reviews. In total, 14 full papers were submitted, of which 12 were accepted (following revision in a second review round), resulting in an acceptance rate of 85%. The accepted papers were presented across four thematic sessions held from July 1 to July 3, 2025, in Vienna.

The organizers would like to express their heartfelt appreciation to the Faculty of Engineering and Computer Science (Fachbereich 2) at the Frankfurt University of Applied Sciences for their generous financial support. We eagerly look forward to the 12th edition of the Spanish-German Symposium on Applied Computer Science, which will take place in Germany in 2026!

Frankfurt am Main, Germany
July 2025

Jörg Schäfer

Organization

General Chair

Elisabeth Orthofer	Technische Universität Graz
Franz Wotawa	Technische Universität Graz

Program Committee Chairs

Jörg Schäfer	Frankfurt University of Applied Sciences, Germany (Chair)
Juan Boubeta-Puig	University of Cádiz, Spain (Co-chair)

Steering Committee

Martin Kappes	Frankfurt University of Applied Sciences, Germany
Inmaculada Medina-Bulo	University of Cádiz, Spain
Francisco Palomo-Lozano	University of Cádiz, Spain
Matthias Wagner	Frankfurt University of Applied Sciences, Germany

Program Committee

Sara Balderas Díaz	University of Cádiz, Spain
Juan Boubeta-Puig	University of Cádiz, Spain
Gregorio Díaz Descalzo	University of Castilla-La Mancha, Spain
Bernabe Dorronsoro	University of Cádiz, Spain
Antonio Garcia-Dominguez	University of York, UK
Gabriel Guerrero	University of Cádiz, Spain
Manuel Méndez Hurtado	Complutense University of Madrid, Spain
Jörg Schäfer	Frankfurt University of Applied Sciences, Germany
Valentin Schwind	Frankfurt University of Applied Sciences, Germany

Barış Sertkaya	Frankfurt University of Applied Sciences, Germany
Martin Simon	Frankfurt University of Applied Sciences, Germany

Additional Reviewers

Christian Baun	Frankfurt University of Applied Sciences, Germany
Anahita Fahrhang	Frankfurt University of Applied Sciences, Germany
Martin Kappes	Frankfurt University of Applied Sciences, Germany
Mercedes G. Merayo	Complutense University of Madrid, Spain
Fatima Sajid Butt	Frankfurt University of Applied Sciences, Germany
Matthias Wagner	Frankfurt University of Applied Sciences, Germany

Can LLMs Detect Equivalent Mutants with Contextual Guidance?

Kevin J. Valle-Gómez[1] and Pedro Delgado-Pérez[2]

[1] University of Cádiz, Cádiz, Spain
kevin.valle@uca.es
[2] University of Cádiz, Cádiz, Spain
pedro.delgado@uca.es

Extended Abstract

The detection of equivalent mutants remains one of the main challenges in mutation testing, both for automated techniques and human practitioners. Despite the versatility of Large Language Models (LLMs), such as ChatGPT, in code understanding tasks, they have achieved only limited success in identifying equivalent mutants reliably [1]. We hypothesise that this limitation may be overcome not through changes to model architecture, but via improved contextual guidance. This work proposes an experimental framework to assess whether structured examples, explicit mutation type definitions, and iterative feedback can enhance LLM performance in this task.

Our approach presents the model with original and mutant versions of source code and asks it to classify the mutant as equivalent or not, while also identifying its mutation category according to a well-established RIP taxonomy (Reachability, Infection, Propagation) [2]. The model must justify its predictions, enabling qualitative analysis of its reasoning processes. We explore the effects of varying the quantity and diversity of examples, transferring guidance across different programs, and introducing correction cycles following prediction errors. The dataset comprises labelled mutants from multiple programs, allowing evaluation through metrics such as precision, recall, F1-score, and confusion matrices.

Although the study is still in a preliminary stage, the proposed design aims to reveal how LLMs internalise program semantics and whether contextual learning generalises across codebases. These findings may help guide future uses of LLMs in mutation testing, and potentially in broader tasks involving program analysis.

References

1. Tian, Z., Shu, H., Wang, D., Cao, X., Kamei, Y., Chen, J.: Large language models for equivalent mutant detection: how far are we? In: Proceedings of the 33rd ACM

SIGSOFT International Symposium on Software Testing and Analysis, pp. 1733–1745 (2024)
2. Yao, X., Harman, M., Jia, Y.: A study of equivalent and stubborn mutation operators using human analysis of equivalence. In: Proceedings of the 36th International Conference on Software Engineering, pp. 919–930. ICSE 2014, ACM (2014)

Contents

Testing

Applications

AI Applications

Testing

An Evaluation of Symbolic Execution for Test Generation in Open-Source C/C++ Software

Martín Nieto-Pinteño, Kevin J. Valle-Gómez(✉), and Inmaculada Medina-Bulo

Departamento de Ingeniería Informática, Universidad de Cádiz, Cádiz, Spain
martin.nietopinteno@alum.uca.es, {kevin.valle,inmaculada.medina}@uca.es

Abstract. Developing software demands strict compliance with high quality and reliability criteria. When dealing with safety-critical systems, where failures can cause severe consequences, these requirements become even more critical, making the testing process especially important and costly in terms of resources. The automated generation of test cases has arisen as a potent method for identifying a greater number of defects while diminishing the need for manual intervention. In particular, Dynamic Symbolic Execution (DSE) has been presented in the literature as an effective technique for the automatic generation of test cases in programs written in C/C++. This work presents a study on its practical applicability in open-source C/C++ projects, using the tools KLEE and gcov to evaluate its effectiveness and the challenges encountered. Additionally, the advantages and limitations of this technique in real-world settings are discussed, along with potential strategies to enhance its applicability.

Keywords: Dynamic Symbolic Execution · Automated Test Generation · Test Case Generation · Static Analysis · Software Testing

1 Introduction

Software development must meet strict quality and reliability standards. In safety-critical systems, where failures can have catastrophic consequences, these requirements become even more demanding, making the testing phase particularly critical and resource-intensive. Automated test case generation has emerged as an effective solution for detecting more bugs with less manual effort. Tools such as EvoSuite [8] and Randoop [11] have shown promising results in Java, where frameworks like JUnit have facilitated widespread adoption. However, in C and C++, the diversity of tools and the lack of a widely adopted standard, despite options such as CppUnit, pose challenges for adopting these techniques, particularly in open-source environments.

Dynamic Symbolic Execution (DSE) has been proposed as a promising approach for automatic test generation in C and C++ [15]. Tools like KLEE [4]

J. Schäfer and J. Boubeta-Puig (Eds.): SGSOACS 2025, CCIS 2831, pp. 3–15, 2026.
https://doi.org/10.1007/978-3-032-14816-2_1

apply this technique to automatically analyse programmes and generate test cases. Nevertheless, applying KLEE to real-world projects introduces significant challenges, including the need to adapt both the code and the build environment, as well as integrating it into projects with multiple dependencies. Although KLEE is designed to explore execution paths in depth, its reference examples are carefully curated and do not reflect the complexity of applying it to large, dependency-heavy codebases. In practice, integrating KLEE into new projects requires setting up a compatible environment, modifying build configurations and, in some cases, making minor code changes to obtain meaningful results.

This work analyses the feasibility of applying DSE to open-source software projects, using KLEE for automatic test case generation. We examine the technical challenges involved in its implementation and evaluate its effectiveness in terms of code coverage, assessing its viability in real-world scenarios.

The rest of this paper is structured as follows: Section 2 details the related work. Section 3 presents the proposed methodology. Then, Sect. 4 presents the case study where the methodology is applied. Moreover, Sect. 5 discusses the results. Finally, Sect. 6 summarizes the conclusions and future work.

2 Related Work

DSE is a software analysis technique that explores multiple execution paths by replacing concrete values with symbolic variables, represented as mathematical constraints. This approach facilitates automatic error detection and test case generation, proving particularly useful in software verification tasks. Its use has enabled the identification of faults such as memory overflows, race conditions, and illegal memory accesses [15].

In the context of C and C++, there are several DSE tools such as Fuzzgrind, KLEE, EXE, DART, CUTE, SAGE, KLOVER and KATCH, with KLEE being one of the most used [4,14]. It operates on *LLVM bitcode*, allowing for exhaustive analysis without executing the code directly. Despite its ability to explore a vast number of execution paths, it faces challenges such as high computational cost and the complexity of analysing code with external dependencies. To assess its effectiveness, coverage tools such as gcov [4] are commonly used to measure which parts of the code are exercised during test execution. Within this context, KLEE has been extensively used in the software verification community [5], establishing itself as a key tool in automating test case generation for C and C++ programmes.

The study carried out on the application of the DSE technique for the automatic generation of test cases provides us with an overview of its relevance and novelty. Among the most interesting publications and research related to the main topic of this work:

- *Scalable Symbolic Execution of Distributed Systems* [7]. It presents a new approach, Symbolic Distributed Execution (SDE), for the application of symbolic execution in distributed systems, where the practical applicability of SDE is generalized and demonstrated with tests in distributed scenarios.

- *KLOVER: A Symbolic Execution and Automatic Test Generation Tool for C++ Programs* [9]. It presents a tool for symbolic execution and automatic test generation for C++ programs and details how the tool is made generic, efficient, and usable for handling real-life industrial applications.
- *KATCH: High-Coverage Testing of Software Patches* [13]. It introduces a technique, whose approach is implemented in a tool, KATCH, for automatically testing software patches, which combines symbolic execution with several heuristics based on static and dynamic program analysis that allow it to reach the patch code.
- *High-Coverage Symbolic Patch Testing* [12]. It proposes an automatic technique, based on symbolic execution, whose purpose is to increase the quality of software patches by providing developers with an automatic mechanism to generate a set of complete test cases that cover as many statements of the patch as possible.

3 Methodology

This work analyses the feasibility of using DSE for automated test generation in open-source C and C++ projects. KLEE is employed as the symbolic analysis tool, and gcov is used to measure code coverage.

To evaluate the effectiveness of KLEE, four open-source projects written in C and C++ were selected, aiming for diversity in structure and complexity, with minimal or well-defined dependencies. The selected projects are *TinyXML2*, *MatrixTCLPro*, *Libarchive* and *Tcpdump* [2], which represent varying levels of complexity and application domains.

The experiment was conducted by compiling each project to *LLVM bitcode* and executing it with KLEE using a general configuration. Coverage was measured with gcov, and practical challenges were analysed, including the impact of dependency management and the computational cost.

For this purpose, an experimental methodology has been developed and it consists of the following steps:

- **Step 1: Adaptation for Dynamic Symbolic Execution**
  Research and implement an adaptation to generate the LLVM bitcodes from the file or library needed for analysis with KLEE.
- **Step 2: KLEE Analysis**
  Design, execute, and analyze the set of test cases using KLEE based on the studied characteristics of the project source code (for example, maximum number of input parameters among the headers of all functions, handling of external or internal files, intervention of standard output stream and intervention of standard input stream).
- **Step 3: Adaptation for Code Coverage Analysis**
  Research and implement an adaptation to generate the necessary information about the source code, using the GCC/G++ compiler, for analysis with gcov.

- **Step 4: gcov Analysis**
  Apply gcov with the right options to obtain information about the source code coverage of the test project's main file and analyze the results.
- **Step 5: Insights, KLEE versus gcov**
  Analyze source code coverage statistics after applying KLEE and gcov, and finally, compare them to discover similarities and differences between the analysis results obtained after applying both tools.

After applying this methodology to the selected projects, preliminary results indicate that KLEE achieves high coverage in small, well-structured projects, but encounters significant difficulties when applying software with multiple dependencies or complex data structures.

While this paper presents a detailed case study focused on the *Libarchive* project, the proposed methodology was also applied to the remaining selected projects. In *TinyXML2* and *MatrixTCLPro*, which feature relatively simple structures and limited dependencies, KLEE achieved code coverage levels close to 80%. By contrast, applying KLEE to *Tcpdump* highlighted significant obstacles due to the project's complexity and extensive reliance on external libraries, resulting in much lower coverage (around 40%) and symbolic analysis processes that exceeded four hours without completion. Further information and detailed results for these projects can be provided upon request.

4 Case Study: Libarchive

Libarchive is a project developing a portable and efficient C library for reading and writing streaming files in various formats. It includes implementations, using the Libarchive library, of common tools such as *tar (bsdtar)*, *cpio (bsdcpio)*, *cat (bsdcat)*, and *unzip (bsdunzip)* [10].

The choice of this project as a test program is due to the complexity of the source code file structure and the configuration provided by the archive that manages the program compilation. This configuration is insufficient, as it does not use the compiler or the appropriate options to generate the LLVM binary code or the necessary information. This initially makes it difficult to adapt and run the project to perform code coverage analysis with KLEE and gcov. Specifically, this case study analyzes the bsdcat tool included in Libarchive.

Step 1: Adaptation for Dynamic Symbolic Execution

Libarchive's complex file structure initially makes adaptation difficult. However, this is simplified by the use of a *Makefile*, which is automatically generated from the project's *CMakeLists* file. *CMakeLists* is a file that this project includes by default, thanks to which and using the *cmake* command the corresponding *Makefile* file will be generated as described in this first step of the proposed methodology in Sect. 3. Once generated, the project can be compiled using the *make* command. In addition, the LLVM extensions and the appropriate compiler are specified to obtain the LLVM binary code and necessary information. Next, we describe the process in detail:

1. Get the project's repository from GitHub. Then, enter the *build* directory of the cloned repository, which may not exist in all projects. When present, it usually contains configuration files and is used as the build directory for compiling the program. As follows:

```
~$ git clone https://github.com/libarchive/libarchive.git
~$ cd libarchive/build
```

2. Update the LLVM *wllvm* extension within a Python virtual environment, which is essential for installing and managing the wllvm tool required to generate LLVM bitcodes for KLEE analysis.

```
~/libarchive/build$ python3 -m venv env
~/libarchive/build$ . env/bin/activate
(env):~/libarchive/build$ python3 -m pip install --upgrade pip
(env):~/libarchive/build$ pip install -U wllvm
```

3. Before extracting LLVM bitcode from the compiled binaries (executables or libraries), you must specify the required compiler and LLVM environment variables. Then, load the configuration into the compilation environment that will be used to compile the program and compile the program. Respectively:

```
(env):~/libarchive/build$ export CC=wllvm && export CXX=wllvm++
(env):~/libarchive/build$ export LLVM_COMPILER=clang
(env):~/libarchive/build$ cmake .. && make
```

4. Finally, enter the *bin* directory, extract the LLVM bitcodes required for subsequent symbolic execution analysis with KLEE, and exit the Python virtual environment:

```
(env):~/libarchive/build$ cd bin
(env):~/libarchive/build/bin$ extract-bc bsdcat
(env):~/libarchive/build/bin$ extract-bc ../libarchive/\
        libarchive.a
(env):~/libarchive/build/bin$ deactivate
```

Step 2: KLEE Analysis

Due to the project's complex file structure, linking the library's LLVM bitcode with the main LLVM bitcode was initially challenging. Using the KLEE option *--link-llvm-lib* allowed the various runs to complete successfully.

This section implements the second step of the proposed methodology. To design the test suite, we studied the source code of the main file (bsdcat.c) and its included headers (bsdcat_platform.h, bsdcat.h, and err.h), following the criteria defined in Step 2 of Sect. 3. The characteristics that determine the different executions are:

- The maximum number of input parameters a function can have in its header. Among all the functions, we get a maximum of 3 input parameters. Therefore, an example of a KLEE argument to include would be *-sym-args 0 3 10*, which creates between 0 and 3 10-byte symbolic arguments.
- The fact that any part of the source code involves internal or external files or that somewhere in the source code the standard output stream operates with some parameter, is not observed in the source code.
- The standard input stream operates on a parameter somewhere in the source code. Although this fact is not observed in the source code, it was included in the tests, since using *--sym-args* alone in KLEE analysis caused execution to pause waiting for *Enter*. To solve this, an example KLEE argument to include would be *--sym-args 0 3 10 --sym-stdin 2048*, which creates between 0 and 3 symbolic arguments of 10 bytes each and converts the standard input stream to a symbolic stream of 2048 bytes.

We ran 12 tests, a set that we found sufficient to evaluate KLEE's code coverage capabilities on the target program. Fewer tests reduced the ability to draw solid conclusions, while additional tests provided little to no improvement in coverage:

```
klee --warnings-only-to-file --only-output-states-covering-new
     --external-calls=all --max-time=3600 --max-solver-time=30
     --write-kqueries --link-llvm-lib=../libarchive/libarchive.bca
     --optimize --libc=uclibc --posix-runtime ./bsdcat.bc <Args>
```

After *./bsdcat.bc*, each test includes symbolic arguments designed to explore as many paths and generate as many test cases as possible. In the Table 1, these arguments (Args) are shown along with the directory where all the information for each test is stored (Path), the number of instructions executed (NI), the total number of completely (CP) and partially (PCP) explored paths and the generated test cases (GTC).

We used the command 'klee-stats klee-out-*' to extract aggregated statistics across the 12 tests.

This command generates Table 2, which summarizes the test suite's source code exploration statistics. The following information is shown for each test: number of instructions explored (Instrs), execution time with KLEE (Time), instruction coverage percentage (ICov), conditional branch coverage percentage (BCov), number of static instructions in the LLVM bitcode (ICount) and the percentage of time that KLEE spent interacting with the Z3 constraint solver (TSolver).

Table 1. KLEE execution info

Path	Args	NI	CP	PCP	GTC
klee-out-0	--sym-args 0 3 10 --sym-stdin 1024	983040	24	2044	61
klee-out-1	--sym-args 0 3 20 --sym-stdin 1024	1003290	25	1651	63
klee-out-2	--sym-args 0 3 10 --sym-stdin 2048	1048576	29	1580	62
klee-out-3	--sym-args 0 3 20 --sym-stdin 2048	1179648	23	1949	69
klee-out-4	--sym-args 0 3 10 --sym-stdin 4096	1319838	37	1735	65
klee-out-5	--sym-args 0 3 20 --sym-stdin 4096	1376256	24	2273	66
klee-out-6	-- test.zip --sym-args 0 3 10 --sym-stdin 1024	4063232	1	1727	55
klee-out-7	-- test.zip --sym-args 0 3 20 --sym-stdin 1024	4128768	1	1839	54
klee-out-8	-- test.zip --sym-args 0 3 10 --sym-stdin 2048	4194304	1	1591	55
klee-out-9	-- test.zip --sym-args 0 3 20 --sym-stdin 2048	4325376	1	1710	54
klee-out-10	-- test.zip --sym-args 0 3 10 --sym-stdin 4096	4128768	1	1599	57
klee-out-11	-- test.zip --sym-args 0 3 20 --sym-stdin 4096	4194304	1	1760	56

Focusing on the test suite statistics shown in Table 2, it is found that the generated test cases covered an average of 28.11% of the conditional branches explored, resulting in an average coverage of 40.83% of the total instructions explored (3.312.5048), in a time of 136.20 seconds, with an average of 89.45% of the time spent interacting with Z3.

Step 3: Adaptation for Code Coverage Analysis

As with the adaptation process for the DSE, the difficulty to adapt Libarchive lies in its file structure, something that is addressed by the Makefile, which is generated from the CMakeLists present in the project directory. Furthermore, the source code must be instrumented to obtain the necessary information by setting the appropriate options in the code compilation and linking environment. In this section, the third step of the methodology proposed in Sect. 3 is developed. It consists of:

1. Assuming the project repository has already been downloaded, create a new directory named *gcovbuild* inside it. This directory will contain a copy of the existing *build* folder, along with a duplicate of the rest of the repository—excluding the *gcovbuild* and *build* directories themselves to avoid recursion or conflicts. Then, navigate into the newly created *gcovbuild* directory:

```
~$ cd libarchive
~/libarchive$ cp -R build gcovbuild
~/libarchive$ cp -R ./!(gcovbuild|build) ./gcovbuild/
~/libarchive$ cd gcovbuild
```

Table 2. klee-stats info. The 'Total (12)' row shows totals for Instrs, Time, and ICount; and averages for ICov, BCov, and TSolver.

Path	Instrs	Time(s)	ICov(%)	BCov(%)	ICount	TSolver(%)
klee-out-0	983040	139.94	39.86	27.47	24587	98.15
klee-out-1	1003290	154.42	40.87	27.79	24587	98.80
klee-out-2	1048576	132.92	42.22	29.62	24587	97.25
klee-out-3	1179648	135.58	41.84	28.65	24587	97.19
klee-out-4	1319838	146.41	40.55	28.12	24587	92.97
klee-out-5	1376256	169.21	40.76	28.51	24587	88.84
klee-out-6	4063232	190.81	40.45	27.61	24587	85.68
klee-out-7	4128768	156.09	42.17	28.80	24587	83.82
klee-out-8	4194304	220.76	39.81	27.36	24587	87.56
klee-out-9	4325376	162.37	40.17	27.54	24587	82.66
klee-out-10	4718592	171.06	40.69	28.08	24587	78.05
klee-out-11	4784128	169.15	40.62	27.72	24587	82.47
Total (12)	33125048	1948.72	40.83	28.11	295044	89.45

2. The **.gcno* files store the count of arc transitions between branches, the count of profiles of specific values taken by variables, and other summary information. They are generated by the flags *-fprofile-arcs* and *-ftest-coverage* when compiling source code with GCC. On the other hand, **.gcda* files store information for reconstructing basic block graphs and assigning source code line numbers to blocks. They are generated when running the product of the previous build [1]. Therefore, it is important to verify that there are no **.gcno* and **.gcda* files which could alter the results, nor *CMakeCache.txt* files which could cause version conflicts:

```
~/libarchive/gcovbuild$ rm -f $(find . -type f \
\( -name "*.gcda" -o -name "*.gcno" \))
~/libarchive/gcovbuild$ rm CMakeCache.txt
```

3. Configure the source code compilation and linking environment, which is used by default by the GCC/G++ compiler, to obtain the *.gcno* files needed for code coverage analysis and compile the program:

```
~/libarchive/gcovbuild$ cmake .. \
  -DCMAKE_C_FLAGS="-fprofile-arcs -ftest-coverage -O0" \
  -DCMAKE_EXE_LINKER_FLAGS="-fprofile-arcs -ftest-coverage -O0"
~/libarchive/gcovbuild$ make
```

Note: you must explicitly use "-O0" so that compiler optimizations do not alter the code handling flow and influence the coverage results.

4. Go to the *bin* directory and run the executable file generated as a result of the compilation to obtain the *.gcda* files, also required for code coverage analysis. In this case, a test file must be passed to the program as an input parameter. Finally, go to the directory where the *.gcno* and *.gcda* files have been generated, and rename them as shown below to be able to perform the analysis with gcov:

```
~/libarchive/gcovbuild$ cd bin && ./bsdcat test.zip
~/libarchive/gcovbuild/bin$ cd ../cat/CMakeFiles/bsdcat.dir
~/libarchive/gcovbuild/cat/CMakeFiles/bsdcat.dir$ mv \
  bsdcat.c.gcno bsdcat.gcno && mv bsdcat.c.gcda bsdcat.gcda
```

Step 4: gcov Analysis

This section corresponds to Step 4 of the methodology (Sect. 3). Once the adaptation is complete, applying gcov is straightforward, as it only requires choosing the correct options (e.g., -abcfHlm) to gather the desired coverage data. Applying the following command produces an output compiled with code coverage information from both the source code files and the header files:

```
~/libarchive/gcovbuild/cat$ gcov -abcfHlm -o \
  ./CMakeFiles/bsdcat.dir bsdcat.c

Function 'main'
Lines executed:62.50% of 24

Function 'bsdcat_read_to_stdout'
Lines executed:71.43% of 14
...
File '/home/user/libarchive/cat/bsdcat.c'
Lines executed:54.24% of 59
Branches executed:74.07% of 27
Taken at least once:40.74% of 27
Calls executed:46.88% of 32
Creating 'bsdcat.c##bsdcat.c.gcov'

Lines executed:54.24% of 59
```

The above output provides detailed coverage information per function, followed by a summary of the overall code coverage for the program. Table 3 presents the coverage data for the functions listed in the previous output, including the method name, percentage of covered executable lines (PELCM), number of executed lines (ELCM), and total executable lines (TELM)

Table 3. Coverage of methods

Method	PELCM(%)	ELCM	TELM
main	62.50	15	24
bsdcat_read_to_stdout	71.43	10	14

We can conclude that 15 (62.50%) of the 24 executable lines in the *main* method are covered, and 10 (71.43%) of 14 in the *bsdcat_read_to_stdout* method.

Table 4 shows the coverage of the file listed in the previous summary, which includes the name of the file (File), the percentage of lines covered with respect to the total executable lines of the file (PELCF), the executable lines covered of the file (ELCF), the total executable lines of the file (TELF), the percentage of covered functions calls with respect to the total functions calls (PFCCF), the covered function calls of the file (FCCF), and the total function calls of the file (TFCCF).

Table 4. Coverage of the program's main file

File	PELCF(%)	ELCF	TELF	PFCCF(%)	FCCF	TFCCF
bsdcat.c	54.24	32	59	46.68	15	32

As shown in Table 4, the file bsdcat.c has 59 executable lines, of which 32 (54.24%) are covered. Additionally, 15 out of 32 function calls (46.68%) are executed. The summary also reports that 74.07% of the 27 conditional branches were evaluated, and 40.74% of them resulted in at least one block being executed. Overall, 54.24% of the file's executable lines are covered.

Step 5: Insights, KLEE versus gcov

In this step, the last of the proposed methodology in Sect. 3, the code coverage obtained after applying KLEE and gcov will be analyzed and compared in order to find similarities and differences between the results obtained.

Table 1 shows that KLEE analyzes all source code instructions for each program, including all executable lines:

- In the most favorable test, *klee-out-2*, the generated test cases cover 29.62% of the explored conditional branches, resulting in 42.22% coverage of the total explored instructions (1048576), in a time of 132.92 seconds, where 97.25% has been dedicated to the interaction with *Z3*.
- In the least favorable test, *klee-out-8*, the generated test cases cover 27.36% of the explored conditional branches, resulting in 39.81% coverage of the total explored instructions (4194304), in a time of 220.76 seconds, where 87.56% has been dedicated to interaction with *Z3*.

Furthermore, it is observed that the fact that a test has executed more or fewer *Instrs* instructions or has dedicated a greater or lesser percentage of time to interaction with Z3 *TSolver*, does not necessarily imply that the test result is better or worse than the others.

KLEE's code coverage remains well below 50%, and the increase in the size of symbolic arguments created by the *--sym-args* option, the inclusion of the *--sym-stdin* option, the increase in the size of the symbolic standard input stream set by the *--sym-stdin* option, and the use of concrete options alongside symbolic options have not significantly improved the result, and have sometimes worsened it.

This limited improvement suggests that coverage issues are not solely due to tooling or configuration, but also reflect deeper limitations of symbolic execution itself. In particular, KLEE may be unable to cover certain execution paths because they require solving complex constraints, involve external system calls, or depend on specific file contents or runtime behavior that symbolic reasoning cannot easily replicate. These algorithmic barriers can limit the effectiveness of DSE even when symbolic input size or runtime is increased.

Knowing that gcov only reports coverage for the files it directly analyzes (rather than the entire program), we observe the following: in the case of *bsdcat.c*, 74.07% of the executable conditional branches were evaluated, and 40.74% had at least one corresponding code block executed. Overall, this resulted in 54.24% coverage of the file's 59 executable lines. This level of coverage is relatively low, as gcov did not exceed 55% in any metric.

Based on the application of the proposed methodology to the selected projects (see Sect. 3), we can conclude that the quality of the individual analyses performed with KLEE and gcov is comparable, provided that the difference in code or instruction coverage between both tools does not exceed approximately 21%.

In the most favorable KLEE test, 42.22% of the LLVM bitcode was covered. Meanwhile, gcov reported 54.24% coverage of the executable lines in the source code. Therefore, considering the values discussed above, we can conclude that both analyses provide a fairly similar level of coverage quality in this case study.

5 Preliminary Results and Discussion

Initial results show that KLEE can generate effective test cases, achieving up to 80% code coverage in small, well-structured projects such as *TinyXML2* and *MatrixTCLPro*. However, its performance degrades significantly in the presence of code complexity and external dependencies. For instance, in *Libarchive* and *Tcpdump*, coverage dropped to around 40% due to interactions with external libraries and the need for specific inputs to reach certain paths.

Another important aspect is execution time. While KLEE can generate test cases in under a minute for smaller programs, symbolic analysis may take several hours due to path explosion. In fact, the symbolic exploration of *Tcpdump* ran for over four hours without completing, which limits the tool's viability in real-world development environments.

These results suggest that, while KLEE can achieve meaningful coverage in controlled scenarios, its applicability to large-scale open-source software presents considerable challenges. Notably, the presence of multiple dependencies and state explosion pose challenges to its scalability. To address these limitations, the literature proposes complementary strategies such as guided *fuzzing* [3] and automated search space reduction [6]. These techniques show potential for improving the exploration of relevant execution paths without excessively increasing computational cost, although their effectiveness in open-source software remains an open challenge.

The experience with KLEE in this study indicates that its effective use requires substantial preparation. It is essential to adapt the build environment, carefully select the functions to be analysed and, in some cases, modify the source code to maximise symbolic exploration. These considerations, observed during the evaluation of projects such as *Libarchive* and *Tcpdump*, are crucial for applying KLEE effectively to real-world software.

6 Conclusions and Future Work

DSE demonstrates strong potential for the automated generation of test cases in software developed in C and C++. Throughout this study, we observed that KLEE can achieve meaningful coverage in projects with well-defined structures and controlled dependencies. However, its applicability to more complex software is limited by path explosion, manual input modelling, and the high computational cost of symbolic execution.

These findings underscore the need for more scalable and efficient DSE techniques to enable their integration into real-world development workflows. In particular, a lack of standardised adoption processes presents a major barrier, especially when compared to the more widespread use of testing tools in languages such as Java or Python. Addressing these limitations may require the evaluation of complementary strategies, such as combining symbolic execution with complementary techniques such as guided *fuzzing* [3] and automated search space reduction [6]. Adapting these strategies to multi-dependency projects could enhance scalability without significantly increasing computational cost.

As future work, we propose developing strategies to ease KLEE's integration into projects with multiple dependencies, minimising the need for manual intervention. We also suggest evaluating the impact of DSE in continuous integration environments, where automated testing must be balanced against time and resource constraints. Additionally, the selective application of DSE to security-critical or fault-prone modules within large projects, rather than analysing the entire codebase, could help mitigate scalability issues while preserving testing effectiveness. These directions will help assess DSE's viability in industrial contexts and its integration into automated pipelines.

Acknowledgments. Grant PID2021-122215NB-C33 (AwESOMe) funded by MICIU/AEI/10.13039/501100011033 and by ERDF/EU.

References

1. Gcov Data Files (Using the GNU Compiler Collection (GCC)) — gcc.gnu.org. https://gcc.gnu.org/onlinedocs/gcc/Gcov-Data-Files.html. Accessed 12 May 2025
2. GitHub - Herramientas para evaluar la aplicación práctica de la herramienta KLEE. https://github.com/Kevus/artefactos-klee-test. Accessed 21 Feb 2025
3. Borzacchiello, L., Coppa, E., Demetrescu, C.: Fuzzing symbolic expressions. In: 2021 IEEE/ACM 43rd International Conference on Software Engineering (ICSE), pp. 711–722. IEEE (2021)
4. Cadar, C., Dunbar, D., Engler, D.R., et al.: KLEE: unassisted and automatic generation of high-coverage tests for complex systems programs. In: OSDI, vol. 8, pp. 209–224 (2008)
5. Cadar, C., Nowack, M.: KLEE symbolic execution engine in 2019. Int. J. Softw. Tools Technol. Transfer **23**, 867–870 (2021)
6. Cha, S., Hong, S., Bak, J., Kim, J., Lee, J., Oh, H.: Enhancing dynamic symbolic execution by automatically learning search heuristics. IEEE Trans. Software Eng. **48**(9), 3640–3663 (2021)
7. Dustmann, O.S.: Scalable Symbolic Execution of Distributed Systems. Ph.D. thesis, Bachelor's Thesis (2010)
8. Fraser, G., Arcuri, A.: A large-scale evaluation of automated unit test generation using evosuite. ACM Trans. Softw. Eng. Methodol. (TOSEM) **24**(2), 1–42 (2014)
9. Li, G., Ghosh, I., Rajan, S.P.: KLOVER: A Symbolic Execution and Automatic Test Generation Tool for C++ Programs. In: Gopalakrishnan, G., Qadeer, S. (eds.) CAV 2011. LNCS, vol. 6806, pp. 609–615. Springer, Heidelberg (2011). https://doi.org/10.1007/978-3-642-22110-1_49
10. Libarchive: Welcome to Libarchive! https://github.com/libarchive/libarchive. Accessed 17 April 2025
11. Liu, X., Yu, P.: Randoop-TSR: random-based test generator with test suite reduction. In: Proceedings of the 13th Asia-Pacific Symposium on Internetware, pp. 221–230 (2022)
12. Marinescu, P.D., Cadar, C.: High-Coverage Symbolic Patch Testing. In: Donaldson, A., Parker, D. (eds.) SPIN 2012. LNCS, vol. 7385, pp. 7–21. Springer, Heidelberg (2012). https://doi.org/10.1007/978-3-642-31759-0_2
13. Marinescu, P.D., Cadar, C.: Katch: High-coverage testing of software patches. In: European Software Engineering Conference/ACM SIGSOFT Symposium on the Foundations of Software Engineering (ESEC/FSE 2013), pp. 235–245 (2013)
14. Chen, T., Zhang, X., Guo, S., Li, H., Yue, W.: State of the art: Dynamic symbolic execution for automated test generation. Futur. Gener. Comput. Syst. **29**(7), 1758–1773 (2013). https://doi.org/10.1016/j.future.2012.02.006
15. Zhang, T., Wang, P., Guo, X.: A survey of symbolic execution and its tool KLEE. Procedia Comput. Sci. **166**, 330–334 (2020)

Refactoring Process as Part of Adapting Test Tools to Real Software

Jose Manuel Heredia-Bravo, Kevin J. Valle-Gómez, M. Carmen de Castro-Cabrera(✉), and Juan José Domínguez-Jiménez

Department of Computer Science and Engineering, University of Cadiz, Av. Universidad de Cádiz, 10, Puerto Real, Cádiz, Spain
{josemanuel.heredia,kevin.valle,maricarmen.decastro, juanjose.dominguez}@uca.es

Abstract. Legacy code is an inherent part of industrial software projects, often resulting in complex, tightly coupled systems that challenge the integration of modern testing techniques. Unlike in academic contexts, where tools are developed with well-scoped objectives and simplified scenarios, industrial environments demand higher levels of robustness, performance, and adaptability. Refactoring, therefore, becomes a crucial process when adapting existing testing tools to support legacy code in production settings. This paper presents the refactoring of a testing tool originally developed for academic use, with the aim of making it compatible with real-world industrial C++ codebases. The project, conducted in collaboration with a naval industry partner, involved reengineering the tool's architecture to improve readability, modularity, and execution performance. Through a case study approach, we illustrate the advantages achieved by systematically applying refactoring principles, resulting in a more robust and adaptable tool capable of supporting automated software testing in complex environments. Additionally, we provide a practical refactoring guide based on our experience, offering valuable insights for teams facing similar adaptation challenges in the future.

Keywords: Refactoring · Software testing · Software engineering · Legacy code · Real-life software

1 Introduction

Bridging the gap between academic tools and industrial requirements remains one of the central challenges in modern software engineering [9]. Tools developed in research contexts are typically designed for controlled environments, assuming simplified codebases, streamlined architectures, and consistent coding styles. In contrast, production-grade software reflects years of iterative development, evolving requirements, and cross-platform constraints. As a result, adapting testing tools originally intended for academic use often reveals substantial limitations when deployed in real-world projects.

J. Schäfer and J. Boubeta-Puig (Eds.): SGSOACS 2025, CCIS 2831, pp. 16–26, 2026.
https://doi.org/10.1007/978-3-032-14816-2_2

These challenges are particularly pronounced in languages such as C++. Its complex memory model, reliance on manual resource management, and absence of native reflection mechanisms present unique obstacles to automated software testing [8]. While solutions exist for managed languages like Java, applying similar techniques to large, legacy C++ systems often proves impractical, especially when dealing with deep inheritance hierarchies, tight coupling, and incomplete documentation.

In this context, refactoring becomes indispensable. Far from being an optional enhancement, it is a prerequisite for making academic tools applicable to industrial environments. Introducing automated testing capabilities into existing tools requires a deliberate redesign focused on improving modularity, maintainability, and scalability. Legacy C++ codebases frequently exhibit issues such as redundancy and non-standard patterns, which must be addressed to ensure robustness and adaptability.

This paper presents the systematic refactoring of a testing tool originally developed within an academic research group, with the goal of enabling its use with industrial C++ software. Initially designed to generate unit test harnesses through static analysis, the tool underwent a comprehensive architectural revision. The case study, conducted in collaboration with a partner from the naval industry, highlights common issues in legacy code and demonstrates how targeted refactoring improved performance, readability, and modularity while preserving the original functionality.

Based on this experience, we propose a practical methodology for adapting academic tools to meet the rigorous demands of industrial applications. The remainder of this paper is structured as follows. Section 2 introduces the software design principles and quality standards that guided our work, and summarizes key contributions in software refactoring. Section 3 describes the transformation process and supporting experiments, while Sect. 4 presents the outcomes and observed improvements. Finally, Sect. 5 offers concluding remarks and outlines future research directions.

2 Background and Related Work

The challenge of bridging the gap between academic software engineering tools and the demands of industrial environments is a persistent one [9]. Academic tools often operate under idealized conditions, contrasting sharply with the complexities inherent in production-grade legacy systems. A key practice in addressing this disparity, particularly when aiming to introduce modern testing techniques, is software refactoring. Consequently, this section defines concepts related to refactoring and summarises some related work.

Refactoring, as defined by Fowler [8], involves modifying the internal structure of software to enhance its understandability and reduce modification costs without altering its observable behavior.

Definition 1. *Refactoring: a change made to the internal structure of software to make it easier to understand and cheaper to modify without changing its observable behavior.*

This concept was notably explored by Opdyke in his thesis [14], focusing on its application within object-oriented programming. Building upon these early investigations into the benefits of restructuring code, the ongoing discussion within the software engineering community highlights the fact that, despite its recognized importance, no dedicated standard exists for refactoring.

Although refactoring lacks a specific and established standard, its importance is widely recognized, prompting discussions on formalizing its practices, including standardized metrics and pattern coding. The significance of refactoring is underscored by its alignment with software quality attributes defined in the ISO/IEC 25000 standard [10], such as maintainability, reliability, and efficiency. By simplifying the code structure, eliminating redundancy, and optimizing logic, refactoring directly contributes to achieving these quality standards.

Definition 2. *Maintainability: capability of a product to be modified by the intended maintainers with effectiveness and efficiency.*

Definition 3. *Reliability: capability of a product to perform specified functions under specified conditions for a specified period of time.*

Definition 4. *Efficiency: capability of a product to use an appropriate amount of resources under stated conditions.*

Another related term is *code smell* defined by Fowler and Beck in [8] as follows: *It is a surface indication that usually corresponds to a deeper problem in the system.*

The body of research on software refactoring is substantial. A comprehensive historical perspective is offered by Abid et al. [5], who review three decades of research in the field, covering various aspects including coverage artifacts, tools, and performance evaluation. Moreover, they provide a repository of publications on the subject and of the main authors. Both highlight current challenges in the field and recommendations for both researchers and software developers in industry. However, in Baqais [7] the focus is on the automation of refactoring, highlighting search-based refactoring as an efficient and recommended technique. Likewise, most papers address code refactoring, and only a few refer to model refactoring.

Tufano et al. analyse the circumstances of when and why code smells are present in the code in [15]. Agnihotri et al. [6] discuss three aspects related to refactoring such as code smells, refactoring techniques (extract method, extract class, and move method, as the most frequent techniques) and software metrics (complexity, coupling, cohesion, and size metrics), highlighting the most common ones. In addition, a list of some tools to automate the detection of smells is included.

Furthermore, refactoring is implicitly supported by agile methodologies, facilitating continuous delivery and adaptability. It embodies the practical application of software design principles like *SOLID* and coding best practices such as *Clean Code*, aiming to improve design quality and maintainability.

The acronym SOLID encapsulates five object-oriented design principles initially defined by Robert Martin [12].

Definition 5 (SOLID principles).

- ***S***—*Single responsibility principle: There should never be more than one reason for a class to change.*
- ***O***—*Open-closed principle: software entities like classes, modules, and functions should be open for extension but closed for modification.*
- ***L***—*Liskov substitution principle: subclasses should be substitutable for their base classes.*
- ***I***—*Interface segregation principle: Many client specific interfaces are better than one general purpose interface.*
- ***D***—*Dependency inversion principle: depend upon abstractions. Do not depend upon concretions.*

Clean code [13] focuses precisely on producing software that is readable, understandable, and easy to maintain over time. The best practices are DRY (Don't Repeat Yourself), KISS (Keep It Simple, Stupid), and YAGNI (You Ain't Gonna Need It). Ljung et al. [11] examined the perception and application of Clean Code principles.

Moreover, refactoring represents the practical application of software design principles (such as SOLID) and coding best practices (such as Clean Code) to existing code. It is an active process of restructuring code to align it with these widely accepted guidelines, with the aim of improving design quality, reducing complexity, and optimizing overall maintainability. By systematically applying these principles through refactoring, developers can mitigate design flaws and create more robust and comprehensible code. In addition, refactoring plays a fundamental role in ensuring adherence to coding standards, thus contributing to code consistency and readability, reducing the probability of errors.

The adaptation of academic tools for industrial use has become an increasingly important topic in software engineering. Garousi et al. [9] discuss the challenges and best practices observed in collaborations between academia and industry, emphasizing the need to evolve research prototypes to meet industrial standards of robustness, scalability, and maintainability. This issue is especially relevant for testing tools, which must integrate seamlessly into complex codebases. In the case of C and C++, despite the availability of frameworks such as GoogleTest [4] and Catch2 [1], automated test generation remains limited, particularly for legacy code. Addressing this gap, our work focuses on refactoring a research tool to enable automated testing in real-world industrial environments.

3 Methodology

This section describes and develops the methodology followed, indicating the stages followed in the refactoring. Furthermore, the analysis carried out, both static and dynamic, and the metrics used to measure the improvements in the tool's code from the initial version to the refactored version are explained.

3.1 Refactoring Process Guidelines

Adapting the tool for industrial environments required a structured refactoring process to address issues related to code quality, maintainability, and integration with industrial-grade software systems. To achieve this, the process was divided into three clearly defined stages: a manual analysis of the existing codebase, the definition of the program execution flow, and a refactoring phase involving code rewriting and the application of design patterns.

1. Manual Code Analysis The main objective of this phase was to gain a comprehensive understanding of the software. Through careful manual inspection, it was possible to identify relevant aspects of the codebase without relying on specialised tools. These included the presence of code smells [8], architectural limitations, the structure and division of the project, class and module responsibilities, and the quality and consistency of internal documentation.

In addition, the analysis revealed a lack of consistent internal documentation. As illustrated in Fig. 1, the header files containing the project's auxiliary functions exhibited poor or incomplete descriptions.

These functions are widely used throughout the codebase, and clear documentation is essential to understand their purpose, return values, and potential side effects. To address this, tools such as Doxygen [3] are commonly employed in software projects due to their widespread adoption and integration with various Integrated Development Environments (IDEs).

Additionally, we analysed the overall structure of the project, which initially lacked a clear and consistent organisational layout. Source files, headers, configuration files, and auxiliary resources were distributed across a flat hierarchy, with little separation of responsibilities or modular grouping. For example, the main directory contained over ten files of mixed types—including code, configuration notes, and documentation—without any clear convention.

2. Execution Flow Definition To fully understand the programme, it was necessary to define its execution flow, capturing essential information such as conditions, loops, outputs, and error handling. An important aspect of this process is that the execution flow remains unchanged before and after the refactoring. In other words, the refactoring process did not introduce new steps, functionalities, or outputs, but rather focused on improving code quality, readability, maintainability, and performance.

```
//Method to check if a file exists given a path
bool fileExists(const string& filename) {
    // ...
}

//Method to check if a file exists given a folder
bool folderExists(const string& folder) {
    // ...
}

//Aux. method to generate the header for the files
string getCommentHeader(string filename) {
    // ...
}

//Given a string and a charater, generates a new string without
  //all the elements before the character.
string deleteAllBeforeChar(string sToReplace, char cToFind) {
    // ...
}

//This method deletes some tags in order to get the types.
  //This was required by the company
string cleanUnnecesaryChars(string sToReplace) {
    // ...
}
```

Fig. 1. Auxiliary functions lack of documentation

For this reason, maintaining a clear representation of the execution flow proved useful. After each refactoring step, it was essential to verify that the program followed the same sequence of operations and produced the same outputs.

3. Refactoring The refactoring process was divided into several steps, designed to be applicable to a wide range of legacy code projects.

Through this structured approach, the tool's codebase was significantly improved in terms of clarity, modularity, and maintainability, while preserving its original functionality and ensuring compatibility with complex industrial C++ code, thus facilitating its adaptation to production environments.

3.1 Refactoring—Project Structure Reorganisation To improve the overall structure of the project, we applied the KISS principle, aiming for simplicity and clarity in directory organisation. Instead of keeping heterogeneous files scattered across arbitrarily named folders, we established a clean and modular hierarchy.

Following the refactoring, the project was reorganised into four main directories: `src` (source files), `include` (header files), `doc` (documentation), and `data` (auxiliary resources). A central `Makefile` and `README.md` were placed at the root to facilitate compilation and orientation.

We also applied SOLID principles. For instance, the Single Responsibility Principle was followed by ensuring that each file encapsulates a single class or functionality, while the Open–Closed Principle was respected by organising features into modular components that can be extended without altering the core logic.

3.2 Refactoring—The Build System The original Makefile presented several problems: rigid structure with hardcoded lists of `.o`, `.cpp`, and `.h` files; unnecessary flags (such as `LLVMCXXFLAGS` and `RTTIFLAG`); and conflicting settings (e.g., `-std=c++0x` together with `-std=c++14`). These violated the YAGNI principle and were removed or simplified.

The refactored Makefile adheres to the KISS principle. It uses generic and automated rules, including the `wildcard` directive to dynamically handle source files.

Additionally, we enabled the `-g` flag, which adds debug information. This makes runtime debugging feasible and aligns with clean code practices by improving error localisation and traceability.

3.3 Code Rewriting At the implementation level, the Single Responsibility Principle was enforced by splitting the original `auxiliary_functions` file into cohesive modules: `utils/checks`, `utils/strings`, `utils/system`, and `utils/templating`. This modularisation promotes clarity and facilitates consistent relative includes.

We also externalised configuration parameters that were previously hardcoded. These are now managed via external JSON files, making the system more adaptable and easier to maintain without recompilation—thus adhering to both the KISS and Open–Closed principles.

Furthermore, the Liskov Substitution and Dependency Inversion principles were implemented through the introduction of a base abstract class `Generator`, extended by concrete classes such as `GTestGenerator`, `CatchGenerator`, and `BoostGenerator`. These classes expose a unified interface for unit test generation, allowing new backends to be added without modifying core logic.

Finally, we decoupled dependencies by eliminating `using namespace` directives from header files and restricting them to implementation files. All utility functions were documented using Doxygen-style comments. A Singleton pattern was also introduced for configuration management, ensuring consistent and controlled access to shared settings across the codebase.

3.2 Metrics Considered

The improvement achieved through the refactoring was measured using static and dynamic analysis tools, in addition to the refactoring steps themselves. On the static side, we compared key metrics such as the number of lines of code and the results of a static code analysis performed using Cppcheck [2], a static code analysis tool for the C and C++ programming languages. Dynamically, we assessed the impact on resource consumption, specifically memory and CPU usage during program execution. In addition, it should be noted that the experiments were carried out on a computer with the following features: Intel Core i7-8565U processor with 1.80 GHZ, 16 GB of DDR4 RAM and a NVIDIA GeForce MX250 graphics card with 2GB of dedicated memory. The device used was a Lenovo ThinkPad T590, operating under WSL 2 with Ubuntu 22.04. The following section presents the findings of these analyses, starting with the static code metrics and analysis results.

4 Discussion and Results

This section details and analyses the findings from the application of the techniques and tools outlined earlier.

First of all, Table 1 illustrates the impact of the refactoring process on the codebase. Although the number of analysed files increased from 16 in the original program to 31 after refactoring, the total number of lines of code saw a significant increase from 3088 to 4099. This indicates that the refactoring process, while potentially improving the structure and maintainability of the code, also led to an expansion in its overall size. Interestingly, the average number of lines per file decreased substantially from 193.00 in the original program to 132.23 after refactoring. This suggests that the refactoring efforts might have involved breaking down larger files into smaller, more manageable units, contributing to a more modular and potentially easier-to-understand codebase, despite the overall increase in the total number of lines.

Table 1. Codebase line count comparison.

Project	Analysed files	Total lines	Average per file
Original program	16	3088	193.00
After refactoring	31	4099	132.23

To assess the impact of the refactoring process on the static analysis of the codebase, we employed the Cppcheck tool. This analysis aimed to identify potential issues related to code style, performance, and potential bugs both before and after refactoring efforts. The results of the static analysis performed by Cppcheck, as detailed in Table 2, highlight a significant reduction in the number of issues detected after the refactoring process. The total number of warnings decreased by 43%, from 68+ to 39, indicating a substantial improvement in code quality and adherence to coding standards. Notably, categories such as 'Unused variables', 'Variable shadowing', 'Unnecessary pass-by-value', and 'Functions that could be `static`' experienced substantial reductions, demonstrating the effectiveness of the refactoring efforts in addressing specific code style and potential performance concerns.

However, the analysis also reveals areas that require more attention. The number of 'Duplicate code (`break`)' instances slightly increased, and a new

'Unused return value' warning appeared after refactoring. These findings suggest that, while the refactoring process successfully eliminated many existing issues, it might have inadvertently introduced or failed to address certain others. Further investigation and targeted refactoring in these specific areas are recommended to achieve an even cleaner and more robust codebase.

Table 2. Cppcheck static analysis results.

Warning type	Original program	After refactoring	Improvement
`style`: Unused variables	7	3	✓ −57%
`style`: Variable shadowing	6	1	✓ −83%
`style`: Duplicate code (`break`)	14	15	× +1 (not yet cleaned)
`style`: Unused functions	13	13	⊖ No change
`style`: Suggested STL algorithms	4	2	✓ −50%
`performance`: Unnecessary pass-by-value	24	3	✓ −88%
`performance`: Functions that could be `static`	4	0	✓ −100%
`warning`: Unused return value	0	1	× +1
Total warnings	**68**+	**39**	✓ **−43%**

The dynamic analysis of resource consumption, summarized in Table 3, reveals interesting trade-offs resulting from the refactoring process. To obtain these results, both the original and refactored programs were executed 5 times over a common test set, and the data presented represents the averages across these executions. The "Refactoring Advantage" column indicates the percentage change (for CPU and Memory) or the percentage reduction (for times and executable size) observed after refactoring. A positive value in this column signifies an improvement, while a negative value indicates an increase or worsening of the metric.

Although the average CPU usage increased slightly from 86.2% to 89.4% after refactoring (a disadvantage of −3.71%), the average real execution time decreased noticeably from 0.51 seconds to 0.42 seconds, representing an improvement of 17.65%. Similarly, the average user and system times also show a reduction of 14.29% and 66.67%, respectively. This suggests that the refactored code might be executing more efficiently in terms of wall-clock time, potentially due to improved algorithms or data structures, even if it demands a slightly higher average CPU utilization.

A significant improvement in memory consumption is observed, with the average memory usage dropping from 97267 KB to 92919 KB after refactoring, indicating an advantage of 4.47%. This indicates that the refactored version is more memory-efficient. However, it's important to note that the executable size increased from 39 MB to 49 MB, representing an increase of −25.64%. This growth in size could be attributed to the introduction of new libraries, more verbose code structures, or additional features implemented during the refactoring. Overall, the dynamic analysis suggests a positive impact on execution time and memory footprint, albeit with a minor increase in CPU usage and a larger executable size.

Table 3. Average resource consumption and executable size comparison.

Metric	Original program	After refactoring	Refactoring advantage
CPU usage	86.2%	89.4%	−3.71%
Real time	0.51 s	0.42 s	17.65%
User time	0.42 s	0.36 s	14.29%
System time	0.03 s	0.01 s	66.67%
Memory usage	97267 KB	92919 KB	4.47%
Executable size	39 MB	49 MB	−25.64%

5 Conclusions and Future Work

Adapting software originally developed in a research environment to meet the demands of industrial use remains a significant challenge. This paper has presented a case study in which a testing tool, initially designed for academic scenarios, was systematically refactored to function reliably in a real-world industrial context.

The work builds upon established refactoring principles and design patterns, as well as widely recognised software engineering standards. The step-by-step process followed throughout the transformation was documented to serve as a practical guide, highlighting the key architectural and structural improvements introduced.

The result is a more readable, maintainable, and modular codebase that preserves the original tool's functionality. This case study illustrates how a structured refactoring approach can bridge the gap between academic prototypes and production-grade software. To support this transformation, static and dynamic analyses were performed. Static analysis showed a notable reduction in code quality warnings, while dynamic analysis revealed improvements in memory usage and execution time, despite a moderate increase in CPU usage and executable size.

Future work will focus on consolidating the refactoring process followed in this case study into a repeatable and transferable methodology. This includes formalising the steps taken, defining selection criteria for refactoring actions, and documenting patterns that proved effective when dealing with legacy C++ code. Such a framework would provide practical guidance for adapting research tools like static analysers or test generators to legacy industrial codebases.

Although the improvements in modularity, documentation, and code quality were substantiated through objective metrics, such as reduced warning counts and improved file structure, some residual issues remain, including duplicated logic and minor unused elements. Refining the process to better detect and address these edge cases is a natural next step. Additionally, applying the approach across a broader set of tools and domains will help validate its generalisability and long-term impact on maintainability.

Acknowledgments. This publication is part of the I+D+i grant PID2021-122215NB-C33(AwESOMe) funded by MICIU/AEI/10.13039/501100011033 and by ERDF/EU, and part of ASSENTER Project PDC2022-133522-I00 funded by MCIN/AEI/10.13039/501100011033 and by the European Union Next GenerationEU/PRTR.

References

1. Catch2. https://github.com/catchorg/Catch2. Accessed 06 May 2025
2. Cppcheck. https://cppcheck.sourceforge.io/. Accessed 14 May 2025
3. Doxygen. https://doxygen.nl/index.html. Accessed 10 May 2025
4. Googletest. https://github.com/google/googletest. Accessed 06 May 2025
5. Abid, C., Alizadeh, V., Kessentini, M., do Nascimento Ferreira, T., Dig, D.: 30 years of software refactoring research: a systematic literature review (2020). https://arxiv.org/abs/2007.02194
6. Agnihotri, M., Chug, A.: A systematic literature survey of software metrics, code smells and refactoring techniques. J. Inf. Proc. Syst. **16**, 915–934 (2020). https://doi.org/10.3745/JIPS.04.0184
7. Baqais, A.A.B., Alshayeb, M.: Automatic software refactoring: a systematic literature review. Software Qual. J. **28**(2), 459–502 (2019). https://doi.org/10.1007/s11219-019-09477-y
8. Fowler, M.: Refactoring: Improving the Design of Existing Code. Addison-Wesley Professional (2018)
9. Garousi, V., Petersen, K., Ozkan, B.: Challenges and best practices in industry-academia collaborations in software engineering: a systematic literature review. In: Information and Software Technology, vol. 79, pp. 106–127. Elsevier (2016) https://doi.org/10.1016/j.infsof.2016.07.006
10. ISO/IEC JTC 1, S.: Systems and software engineering — Systems and software Quality Requirements and Evaluation (square) — Guide to square. Standard, International Organization for Standardization (2014)
11. Ljung, K., Gonzalez-Huerta, J.: "to clean code or not to clean code" a survey among practitioners. In: Taibi, D., Kuhrmann, M., Mikkonen, T., Klünder, J., Abrahamsson, P. (eds.) Product-Focused Software Process Improvement, pp. 298–315. Springer International Publishing, Cham (2022)
12. Martin, R.: Design principles and design patterns. Object Mentor **1**(34), 597 (2000)
13. Martin, R.C., Coplien, J.O.: Clean Code: A Handbook of Agile Software Craftsmanship. Prentice Hall, Upper Saddle River, NJ (2009)
14. Opdyke, W., Johnson, R.: Refactoring object-oriented frameworks (1992)
15. Tufano, M., Palomba, F., Bavota, G., Oliveto, R., Di Penta, M., De Lucia, A., Poshyvanyk, D.: When and why your code starts to smell bad. In: Proceedings of the 37th International Conference on Software Engineering, vol. 1, pp. 403–414. ICSE '15, IEEE Press (2015)

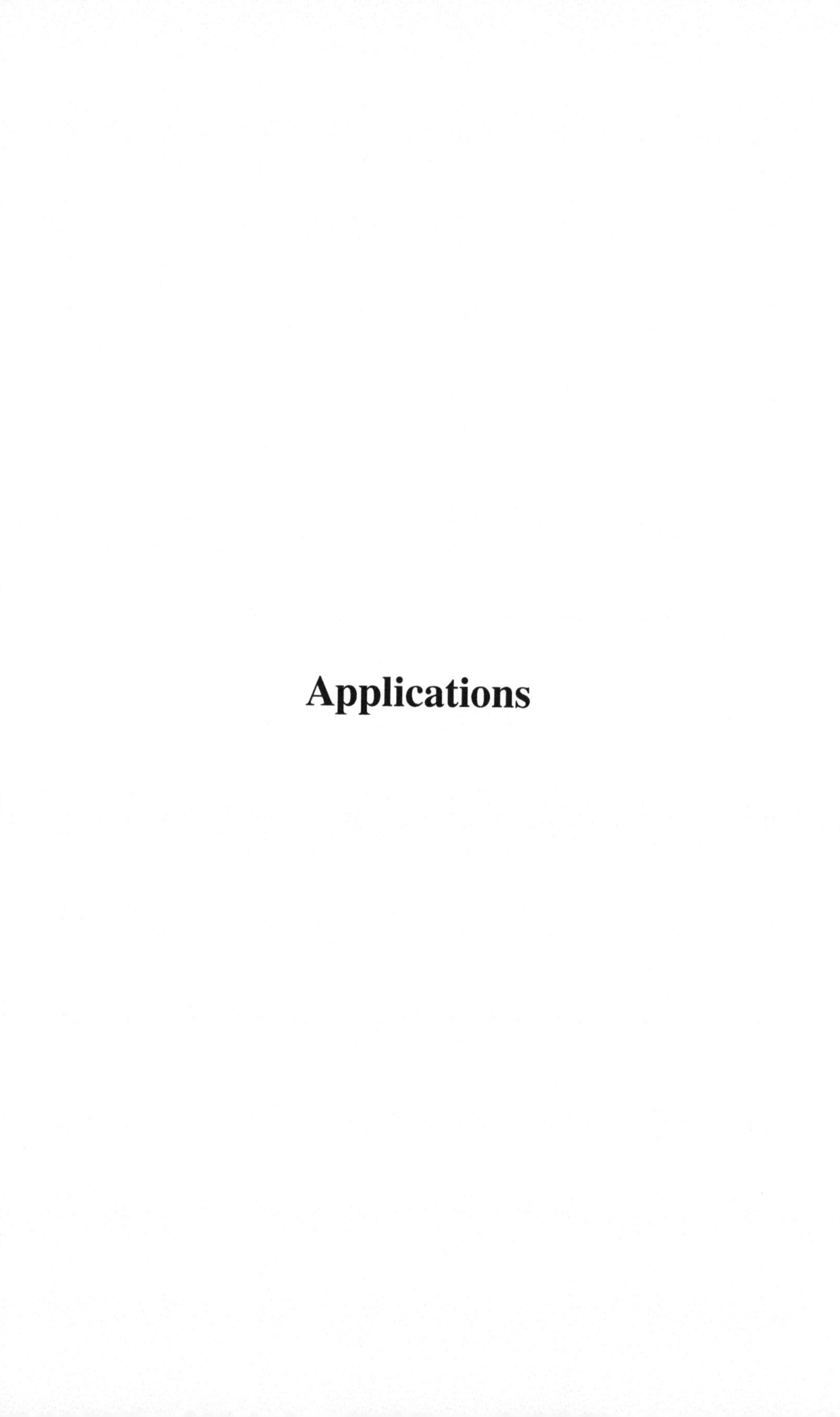

Applications

An Ontology for Climate Risks in a Credit Risk Management Framework for Financial Institutions

Hendrik Weichel[1,2(✉)], Jürgen Angele[3], George Baryannis[2], Jörg Schäfer[1], Barış Sertkaya[1], Martin Simon[1], and Ann Smith[2]

[1] Frankfurt University of Applied Sciences, Frankfurt am Main, Germany
hendrik.weichel@fb2.fra-uas.de

[2] University of Huddersfield, Huddersfield, UK

[3] adesso-Competence Center Artificial Intelligence, Dortmund, Germany

Abstract. Climate-related risks have recently emerged as critical factors in financial risk management, resulting in significant demand for reliable and standardized sustainability data. In response, the European Union (EU) has established regulatory frameworks mandating corporations of varying sizes to disclose key sustainability indicators. These developments facilitate improved quantitative risk management through consistent and accessible sustainability data published by corporations in their respective reports. However, reporting from diverse and heterogeneous data sources necessitates structured methods for storing and organizing domain knowledge, enabling efficient data access and retrieval.

To address these challenges, we introduce an ontology designed to function as a schema for constructing a Knowledge Graph (KG) that integrates data essential for assessing climate risks within financial institutions' loan portfolios. Following established ontology modeling practices, our approach reuses and extends existing ontologies, ensuring alignment with the latest EU reporting standards specified in the Corporate Sustainability Reporting Directive (CSRD). This ontology, which is made publicly available, supports the assessment of transition climate risks, e.g., through a portfolio temperature alignment framework and further enhances capabilities for information extraction, identification of data gaps, and analysis of data integrity within sustainability reports.

Keywords: Ontology · Knowledge Graphs · Sustainable Finance · Climate Risks · Information Extraction

1 Introduction

In recent years, financial institutions have increasingly recognized the necessity of integrating climate-related risks into their credit risk management frameworks, driven partly by regulatory developments such as the Guidelines on the management of climate risks by the European Banking Authority (EBA) and the EU

J. Schäfer and J. Boubeta-Puig (Eds.): SGSOACS 2025, CCIS 2831, pp. 29–43, 2026.
https://doi.org/10.1007/978-3-032-14816-2_3

Corporate Sustainability Reporting Directive (CSRD). A critical challenge in this integration is the effective representation and utilization of domain-specific knowledge about climate risks, which often spans heterogeneous data sources with complex interdependencies. In particular, significant gaps persist in the availability and quality of Scope 3 emissions data, complicating accurate climate risk assessments.

Ontologies offer a robust solution to these challenges by providing structured, explicit, and formal representations of domain knowledge, facilitating interoperability, data retrieval, reasoning, and inference. In this paper, we propose an ontology explicitly designed to model domain knowledge regarding climate risks within the context of credit risk management for financial institutions. The proposed ontology facilitates the identification of data gaps, uncertainty, and enables consistency checks across diverse data sets. Moreover, we establish a connection to extracting and structuring relevant information from unstructured data sources, highlighting how the ontology enhances these processes by providing clear semantic context. Guided by foundational principles such as modularity and reusability, our approach extends and integrates established ontologies from both industry practices and academic research. We extend the Ontosustain ontology [1,2], a recent modeling approach of the regulations mandated by the CSRD, and integrate it within the Financial Industry Business Ontology (FIBO)[1], which is considered standard in the financial industry [3]. This purposefully designed approach ensures compatibility and ease of integration into existing systems, aligning closely with regulatory requirements and reporting expectations. Ultimately, the developed ontology serves as a foundational schema, paving the way toward the construction of comprehensive Knowledge Graphs (KGs). These KGs, empowered by semantic technologies, have the potential to significantly enhance the ability of financial institutions to understand, manage, and mitigate climate-induced credit risks. Moreover, our work supports the ongoing integration of Large Language Models (LLMs) into the workflows of financial institutions. Ontologies and LLMs complement each other effectively: on the one hand, LLMs can assist in developing and refining ontologies; on the other hand, ontologies can serve as a regularizer, providing structured context to enhance LLM performance.

The remainder of this paper is structured as follows: Sect. 2 provides an overview of the advantages of ontologies and their synergy with LLMs, along with a summary of existing ontologies in the sustainable finance domain. In Sect. 3, we present a credit risk management use case based on portfolio temperature alignment. Building on this use case, the ontology is developed using MOMo, as described in Sect. 4, and subsequently validated in Sect. 5. Section 6 concludes the paper and outlines directions for future research, while Sect. 7 discusses the limitations of the present study.

---

1 https://www.edmcouncil.org/frameworks/industry-models/fibo/.

2 Related Work

Ontologies provide a unified interface to the accumulated knowledge within a specific application domain by ensuring coherent use of terminology and by describing the relationships and dependencies between object classes. In combination with reasoning, ontologies play a key role in modeling application domains, detecting inconsistencies, and explaining unwanted consequences. They have proven successful in modeling tasks in several fields including biology, medicine, and software engineering. KGs [4] rely on ontologies for schema definition and provide the technological background of several modern Artificial Intelligence (AI) applications and intelligent assistance systems. They enable the integration of data from heterogeneous data sources on a large scale. Due to their simple yet elegant and scalable way of storing data, they have gained significant attention in recent years both in industrial applications and in academic research. Google, for instance, uses its Google KG to improve semantic search [5]. Amazon helps its customers find products easily using its product graph [6]. In addition to these commercial KGs, there are promising public KGs like DBpedia [7], WikiData [8] and YAGO [9] that are used in various AI applications that depend on robust modeling of data and information.

Furthermore, rules and logic can improve an ontology's expressiveness. This allows automated reasoning, consistency checking, and more powerful querying, ultimately improving data integration, interpretation, and decision-making. One approach that is prominent in the industry is OO-logic [10,11]; it combines the concepts of object-orientated modeling with the declarative style, compact and simple syntax, and stratified semantics of a first order logic-based language (Horn logic plus negation). OO-logic runs on a system called *SemanticReasoner*. Its rule based language provides over 200 built-ins from Java Math and String library and a lot more which was very important for implementing applications. This set of builtins contains so called Connectors to other systems allowing easy integration of external data during run-time. Moreover, the set of builtins is easily extendable. Besides OO-logic *SemanticReasoner* provides GraphQL as query language. *SemanticReasoner* is also a vector store which allows a nice combination of powerful meta modeling, rules and search in the vector store for GraphRAG applications.

The ability of KGs and ontologies to model real-world knowledge in a explicit machine-readable format serves as a powerful complement to LLMs, which store knowledge implicitly in their parameters [12,13]. LLMs show great performance in processing natural language, but lack in decisiveness and are prone to hallucinations. KGs are an easily-accessible data storage that can enhance LLMs performance in multiple ways: their explicit modeling of knowledge enables improved explainability, they can help identify knowledge gaps by exploiting logical facts, and they can facilitate data augmentation for LLMs through better information retrieval (this approach is known as GraphRAG [14]). Furthermore, KGs can enhance information extraction through providing additional prior knowledge [15], enabling reciprocal interplay of LLMs and KGs: LLMs can help populate a KG and the resulting KG provides knowledge to make LLM-based information extraction more robust.

Prior work in the field of financial ontology modeling has examined integrating sustainability standards into an ontology for more comprehensive data collection and organization: [16,17] model standards of the Global Reporting Initiative (GRI)[2], one of the most widely used sustainability reporting frameworks. Both works were published before the introduction of the European Sustainability Reporting Standards (ESRS)[3], the official standards that resulted from the CSRD. Zhou and Perzylo present the Ontosustain ontology [1], an ontology specifically designed to support the internal organization of sustainability data within small and medium-sized enterprises. It was designed based on the GRI and the ESRS. Usmanova and Usbeck [2] extend OntoSustain by incorporating qualitative data points from the ESRS 2 topical standards, which represent climate-related disclosures from companies' annual reports. This provides a foundational step for modeling sustainability reporting in KGs. However, the authors primarily focus on narrative (textual) reporting and omit quantitative data points, which are essential for comprehensive, quantitative risk management. Moreover, they also explore populating the ontology using LLMs.

The Financial Industry Business Ontology (FIBO)[4] is the largest reference standard for retail, commercial, and investment banks. It models financial contracts, product and service specifications, as well as governance and regulatory documentation, and includes specific modeling of commercial loans[5]. FIBO is regularly updated and has been reused in other financial modeling efforts, such as the Bank Ontology[6]. However, it currently lacks classes representing corporate sustainability reporting.

3 Taking the Temperature of a Loan Portfolio: An Illustrative Credit Risk Management Use Case

Credit risk management in financial institutions is the process of identifying, assessing, and mitigating the risk that borrowers (individuals, companies, or governments) will fail to repay their loans or meet contractual obligations. It is a crucial function to ensure that banks remain financially stable and avoid significant losses. Climate risk, which is commonly divided into transition risk (due to, e.g., changes in regulations, technologies, or market preferences during the shift to a low-carbon economy) and physical risk (caused by, e.g., extreme weather events or long-term environmental shifts) is an additional driver to the existing classical credit risk subcategories: default risk, downgrade risk, spread risk, and recovery risk. Over the past years, Portfolio Temperature Alignment has become an essential metric for financial institutions seeking to quantify and

[2] https://www.globalreporting.org.
[3] https://www.efrag.org/en/sustainability-reporting/esrs-workstreams.
[4] https://www.edmcouncil.org/frameworks/industry-models/fibo/.
[5] https://www.spec.edmcouncil.org/fibo/ontology/LOAN/LoansGeneral/Loans/.
[6] https://www.bankontology.com.

manage climate-related transition risks, enabling alignment of investment strategies with global climate targets such as those established by the Paris Agreement. The X-Degree Compatibility (XDC) metric, developed by the Frankfurt-based climate-tech company right° [18], provides a scientifically robust calculation of an economic unit's contribution to global warming. The significance of such approaches was recently emphasized in a European Banking Authority (EBA) Staff Paper [19], which uses the XDC metric to illustrate how financial institutions can assess the alignment of their loan portfolios with climate targets. Specifically, the authors state: "[...] we argue in this paper for a complementary perspective beyond prudential supervision, namely banks' own contribution to global warming through their financing of climate-harmful activities. This perspective becomes especially relevant considering the prospective reporting on double materiality according to the EU Corporate Sustainability Reporting Directive (CSRD). [...] Additionally, we show that the implied temperature rise as per our methodology can also serve as proxy for transition risk [...]"

Computing the XDC metric for an economic entity, such as a company, requires several input data points: greenhouse gas emissions and the company's transition plan, mandated by the CSRD, including specific emission-reduction milestones; the industrial sectors in which the company operates; and key financial figures such as EBITDA, gross value added (GVA), and employee costs. Furthermore, integrating the XDC metric (as a proxy for transition risk) into traditional credit-risk frameworks additionally requires general loan terms and conditions, including the loan amount, maturity, and repayment schedule.

One of the major challenges in quantifying climate risk is the uncertainty inherent in both climate predictions and input emission data. In particular, reported emissions data can undergo substantial revisions in subsequent reports, sometimes varying by more than 50%. Such revisions typically occur when companies shift from a spend-based method to a more precise, activity-based method for measuring Scope 3 emissions. Activity-based methods rely on detailed physical data, such as actual quantities of goods produced, transported, or consumed, rather than purely financial expenditure data. While these methodological shifts improve accuracy, they introduce significant volatility into historical emissions data, complicating trend analyses and risk assessments. Consequently, robust quantification of climate-related transition risks demands careful treatment of these uncertainties, as demonstrated, for example, in a recent work [20]. The ontology presented here is particularly well-suited to support such approaches.

4 Methodology

We apply the MOMo methodology [21,22] to develop an ontology that serves as a schema for a KG tailored specifically to banking and financial institutions, with a particular focus on transition climate risks within credit risk management, as detailed in Sect. 3. MOMo was selected due to its modular design principles and the availability of promising existing ontologies identified for reuse in our preliminary research. In the following sections, we highlight key aspects of the ontology's development. A comprehensive overview of MOMo and its application to our project is provided in Appendix A.

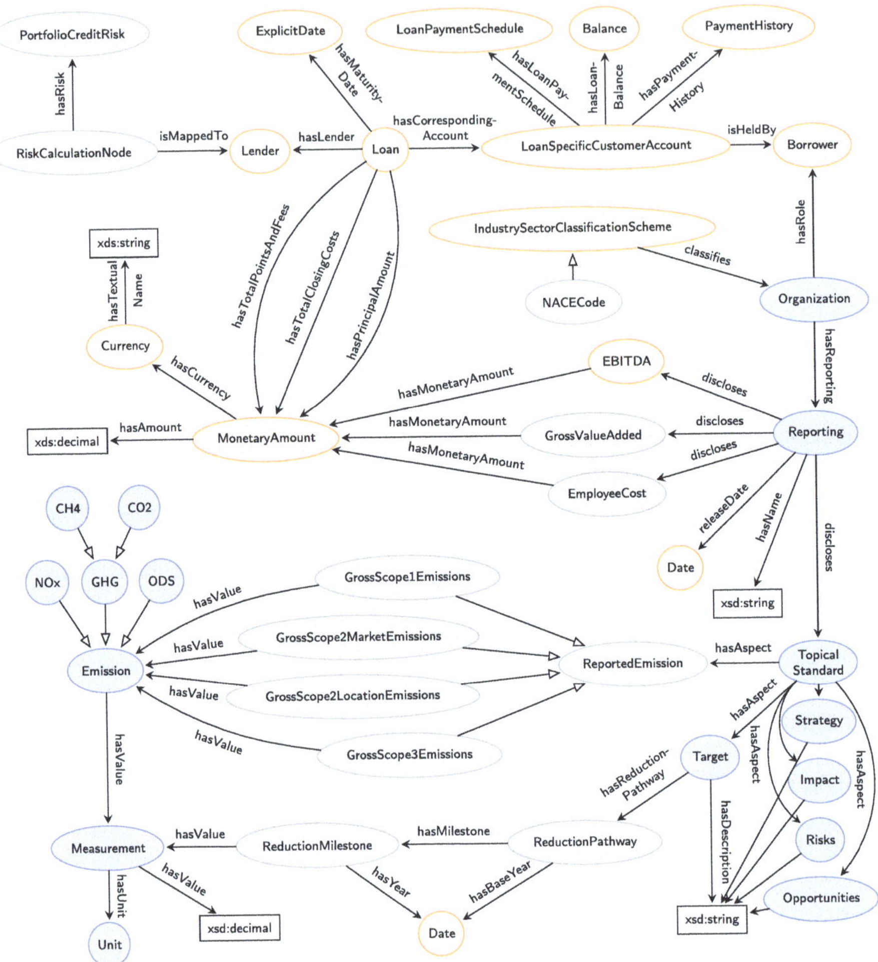

Fig. 1. Proposed Ontology for modeling Climate Risks in a Credit Risk Management Framework for Financial Institutions. Blue classes come from the extended Ontosustain, Orange classes come from FIBO, and gray classes are new. (Color figure online)

4.1 Use-Case Description

The use-case description for the ontology is the following:

"Build an ontology that can be used in financial institutes to assess the data required for modeling the climate risks in commercial loans. The data for this modeling is defined in the ESRS and includes information about companies, including emissions, their sustainability targets, and assessment about the compatibility of their business model with climate change targets. Additionally, it requires financial data from the borrowers, such as Earnings Before Interest, Taxes, Depreciation, and Amortization (EBITDA) and employee compensation, as well as the company's classification within industrial sectors."

4.2 Competency Questions

From the use-case description and in consultation with domain experts, we derive a set of competency questions. This is a standard procedure in ontology design [23], and the second step of the MOMo methodology.

CQ1 What loans comprise the full lending portfolio of a particular bank?
CQ2 What are the terms and conditions of the loan (monetary amount, run time, interest, repayment schedule)?
CQ3 What climate-related risks, opportunities, and targets did the borrower identify in their business model?
CQ4 What industry-sectors does the borrower participate in?
CQ5 What is the Gross Value Added (GVA), which is the sum of EBITDA, and the costs for employees, of the borrower?
CQ6 Represented in a machine-readable pathway, what decarbonization targets does the borrower have?
CQ7 What were the gross Scope 1, Scope 2 Location, Scope 2 Market, and Scope 3 emissions of the borrower in recent years?
CQ8 What is the time series of sustainability reports over the last years?
CQ9 Do the reported financials reflect the transition plan?

We identify two types of data sources relevant to these competency questions: (1) data vendors and (2) borrowers' direct publications, such as annual or sustainability reports. Structured data from vendors can be automatically integrated into ontologies by translating them into semantic representations aligned with ontology concepts and relationships. In contrast, data from annual reports, typically provided as unstructured PDFs, must be extracted either manually or automatically, as demonstrated, for instance, in [2,15].

4.3 Key Notions, Patterns Identification, and Module Diagrams

From the competency questions above, we infer the notions *Loan*, *Loans' Conditions*, *Borrower*, *Financial Reports*, and *Sustainability Reports*. We selected the notions *Loan* and *Borrower* as key notions. *Loan* models the credit agreement between a borrower and a lender with the terms and conditions of the loan. The *Borrower* notion models the company that applies for a loan with all the necessary data to assess its creditworthiness. Following reusability and modularity as key practices of ontology modeling, we reuse existing ontologies to model each key notion.

Loan. Specifically CQ1 and CQ2 require modeling the loan agreements between the lender, potentially a bank, and its borrowers. To model this key concept, we adopt a relevant subset of FIBO, given that it is comprehensive and widely used in the financial domain. The corresponding entities are shown in Fig. 2.

In addition to the classes from FIBO, we added a *RiskCalculationNode* that serves as the connection between a lender and its *PortfolioCreditRisk* which describes the risk involved in lending money to the borrowers. This procedural modeling is needed to align with Ontosustain, as described later.

To obtain this subset of classes from FIBO, we used the ROBOT tool [24], specifically the function `extract` with the method `BOTTOM`. ROBOT is a lightweight tool that facilitates automated modularization of RDF and OWL files. This generates a balanced ontology that includes all classes and relations that are required for our use case.

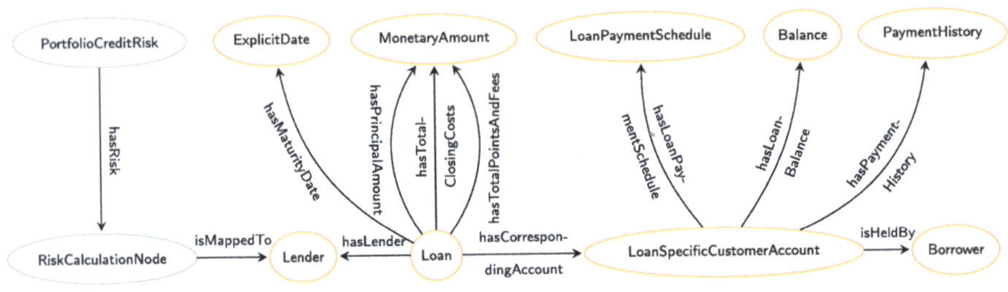

Fig. 2. The key notion of loans. Orange classes come from FIBO, and gray classes are new. (Color figure online)

Borrower. In a loan or credit agreement, the borrower is the party seeking to borrow money from a bank. In commercial loans, this borrower is usually a company. We model the key notion *Borrower* in association with the notions *Financial Reports* and *Sustainability Reports*; this provides responses to competency questions three through nine. Altogether, this key notion provides the data required to assess the credit risks that the lender has to bear.

To model the *Borrower* key notion, we build on top of the extended version of Ontosustain proposed by Usmanova and Usbeck [2]. Ontosustain models company internal processes and data that support the creation of sustainability reports with sustainability indicators from ESRS 1 standards. The extension by Usmanova and Usbeck also includes general disclosures from ESRS 2, by incorporating a *Reporting* class that represents a reporting of sustainability disclosures through, e.g., an annual report. This includes the disclosure of decarbonization targets, strategies and the impact, risks, and opportunities of climate change that affects the business model, answering CQ3. The core class of Ontosustain is Organization, representing companies and corporations of all sizes. We adopt this class to represent organizations and connect it through a *hasRole* relation with the *Borrower* class related to the *Loan* key notion. Looking at the competency questions, we identified the following gaps in the extended Ontosustain ontology: CQ4 requires assessing the NACE code, the Statistical Classification of Economic Activities in the European Community, for each industry sector the organization participates in. We add a class *NACECode* that has a relation *identifies* to the class *Organization*. When merging both key notions, we can see that this class is a subtype of the *IndustrySectorClassificationScheme* class in FIBO. CQ5 asks for financial key figures of the borrower, namely the Gross Value Added (GVA) which is calculated from EBITDA, and the costs for employees. We model all these three key measures as a disclosure in the *Reporting* class. They all have an *MonetaryAmount* which consists of a quantity and a currency. CQ6 requires the decarbonization targets of a company. In the extended Ontosustain ontology, these targets are modeled as descriptions in string format. This modeling is not feasible in quantitative risk management; to address this, we extend the class *Target* by adding a *ReductionPathway* that refers to several *ReductionMilestones*. Each reduction milestone specifies a target at a particular point in time, aiming to reduce the company's emissions either to an absolute level or to a level relative to a defined base year. CQ7 requires the Scope 1, Scope 2 Location, Scope 2 Market, and Scope 3 emissions of the borrower over the recent years. Location-based emissions are calculated using the average emissions intensity of the electricity grid, and market-based emissions are calculated using emission factors from the particular electricity suppliers. To fulfill this requirement, we add the corresponding data points to the *TopicalStandard* class that comes from the ESRS E1-6 standard[7]. Reported emission data consist of quantitative measurements expressed in specific units, typically carbon dioxide equivalent tonnes (CO2e) and corresponding numerical values. To model these emissions, we utilize the *Measurement* class provided by OntoSustain. While this approach adequately addresses our current use case, more detailed modeling of physical units might be required for complex scenarios.

A notable feature of our emission data modeling approach is that each report is associated with a reporting date. This enables the creation of temporal subgraphs originating from the reporting node, facilitating time series analyses of emission data. Such analyses support the evaluation of reporting quality and detection of inconsistencies across reports, directly addressing competency questions CQ9 and CQ8.

4.4 Creating the Final Ontology

We model the ontology such that the *Organization* class can take the role of a borrower through a *hasRole* relation. The full ontology can be seen in Fig. 1. Blue classes come from the extended Ontosustain ontology, Orange classes come from FIBO, and gray classes are newly introduced. The initial version of the ontology is publicly available online[8]. Appendix B provides a step-by-step analysis of the ontology creation process.

7 https://xbrl.efrag.org/e-esrs/esrs-set1-2023.html.

8 https://github.com/hendrikweichel/ontology_climate_credit_risks.

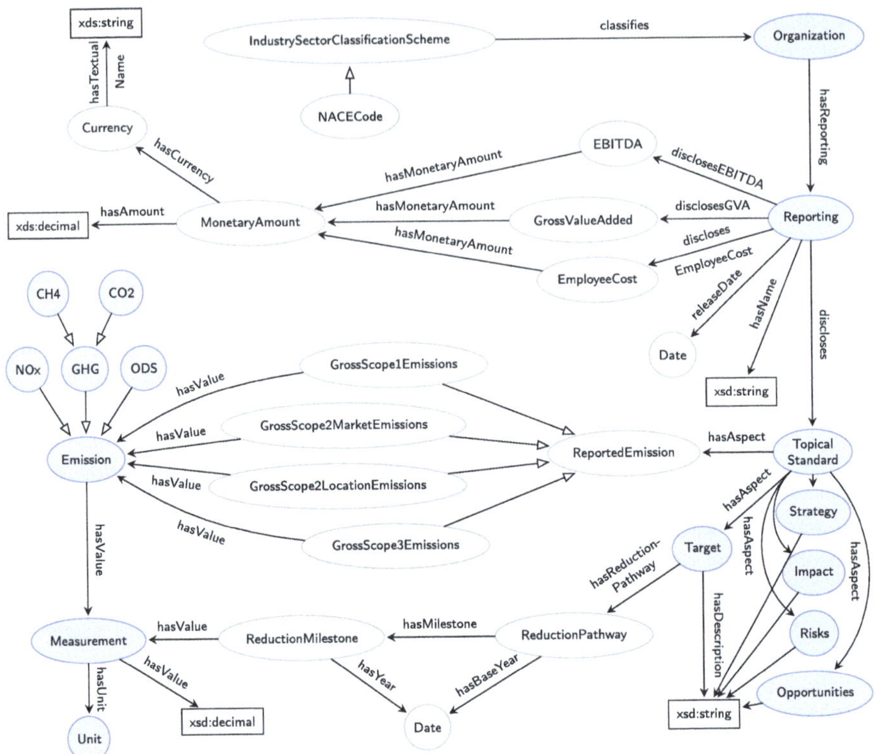

Fig. 3. The key notion of organization. Blue classes come from the extended Ontosustain ontology, and gray classes are added manually. (Color figure online)

5 Validation

To confirm the validity of this ontology, we conducted an expert validation in which the expert and ontology engineers jointly reviewed its completeness and suitability by verifying that all competency questions can be answered using the ontology's classes and relations.

Let us illustrate the ontology's validity by validating two representative competency questions and show how to answer them by providing SPARQL queries: CQ1, "*What loans comprise the full lending portfolio of a particular bank?*", can be queried with the following SPARQL statement for a lender entity <Bank>:

```
SELECT ?loan
WHERE {
    ?loan :hasLender :<Bank> .
}
```

CQ7, "*What were the gross Scope 1, 2, and 3 emissions of the borrower in recent years?*", can be answered for the borrower organization <Borrower> through the following query:

```
SELECT ?value ?unit ?date ?emissionType
WHERE {
    ?Organization :hasRole :<Borrower> ;
                  :hasReporting ?Reporting .
    ?Reporting :discloses :?TopicalStandard ;
               :releaseDate :?date .
    ?TopicalStandard :hasAspect :?ReportedEmission .
    ?ReportedEmission a :GrossScope1Emission .
    ?GrossScope1Emission :hasValue :?Emission .
    ?Emission :hasValue :?Measurement .
    ?Measurement :hasValue ?value ;
                 :hasUnit ?unit .
    ?ReportedEmission rdf:type ?emissionType .
}
```

6 Conclusion and Future Work

In this study, we presented an ontology for modeling and conceptualizing corporate sustainability reports, addressing the use case of credit risk management using a portfolio temperature alignment approach. To the best of the authors' knowledge, this ontology represents the first publicly available resource tailored specifically for this domain and use case. The ontology provides a foundation for developing robust information-extraction frameworks that integrate LLMs, enabling financial institutions to systematically incorporate quantitative climate risk analysis into their credit risk assessments, supported by high-quality data.

In future work, the expressive power of the ontology will be enhanced through the addition of a dedicated rule and logic layer [10,11]. This extension will offer two significant advantages. First, rules can automatically validate incoming data, typically provided by a data input pipeline, ensuring consistency with the ontology's underlying logic. Any data conflicting with these rules will trigger an immediate error. Second, integrating a logic layer will enable the ontology to directly infer domain-specific knowledge. At present, external applications must query the ontology via SPARQL to retrieve data required for risk assessments. In contrast, a built-in logic layer could internally perform these risk assessments and expose the results through an API, thereby increasing the ontology's expressiveness and reducing reliance on external applications.

7 Limitations

A notable limitation of this research is that the modeling of climate risks specifically targets the portfolio temperature alignment approach. Other climate risk management methodologies may require additional or different knowledge representations within the ontology. Moreover, implementing comprehensive climate risk management critically depends on the availability of high-quality data. Ensuring data quality necessitates regulatory oversight to mitigate risks of manipulation or misconduct.

Acknowledgments. This project (HA project no. 1647/23-200) is financed with funds of LOEWE – Landes-Offensive zur Entwicklung Wissenschaftlich-ökonomischer Exzellenz, Förderlinie 3: KMU-Verbundvorhaben (State Offensive for the Development of Scientific and Economic Excellence). Martin Simon would like to acknowledge support by the German Federal Ministry of Education and Research (BMBF) under Grant No. 03FHP191.

Disclosure of Interests. The authors have no competing interests to declare that are relevant to the content of this article.

A Modular Ontology Modeling (MOMo) Methodology

The Modular Ontology Modeling (MOMo) Methodology is a methodology designed to create ontologies with an emphasis on modular design and Ontology design patterns (ODPs). The methodology comprises ten steps that lead to the formalization of an ontology in the context of a real-world use case. It finally aims to create an OWL file containing triplets and axioms of an ontology. We simplified this workflow since we only create an RDF ontology, these were the steps. Table 1 summarizes MOMo as presented in [21].

Table 1. MOMo workflow in [21]

Step	Responsible	Output
1. Describe use cases & data sources	Entire team	Use case descriptions
2. Gather competency questions	Entire team	List of CQs
3. Identify key notions	Entire team	List of key notions
4. Identify existing ODPs	Ontology engineers	Selected ODP(s) for each key notion
5. Create module diagrams	Entire team	Diagrammatic representation of the solution module
6. Document modules & axioms	Ontology engineers & domain experts	Module documentation with embedded schema diagrams, axiomatization
7. Create ontology diagram	Ontology engineers	Diagrammatic representation of the whole composed ontology
8. Add spanning axioms	Ontology engineers	Documentation of the entire ontology with embedded schema diagrams, axiomatization
9. Review naming & axioms	Ontology engineers	Updated module and ontology documentation
10. Create OWL file & axioms	Ontology engineers	An OWL file for publication and use

B Procedure for RDF Domain Creation

The step-by-step application of MOMo for our purposes is described below. Note that, for the development of the initial version, we have not focused on axiomatization.

1. Get the required subset of FIBO *Loans General*[9] using the extract functionality of the tool ROBOT [24].
2. Import the subset of the FIBO ontology.
3. Add *PortfolioCreditRisk* as a subclass of *Risk* and *RiskCalculationNode.*
4. Implement the Ontosustain ontology (including Reporting extension) in RDF, since there is no open RDF source (some classes which are not relevant for our project were omitted).
5. Import Ontosustain including reporting extension.
6. Extend Ontosustain with:
   (a) Scope 1, Scope 2 Market, Scope 2 Location, and Scope 3 Emissions.
   (b) Pathway for climate targets.
   (c) NACE code node.
   (d) EBITDA node.
   (e) Employee cost node.
7. Connect both notions over *hasRole* relation between *Organization* and *Borrower.*
8. Entity mapping of both notions:
   (a) As *Organization* exists in both FIBO and Ontosustain, model their equivalence.
   (b) *EBITDA* is available in both notions, unify them.
   (c) Model *EBITDA* and *Employee Cost* as subtypes of *Specification and Expression* from FIBO.
   (d) *Monetary amount*, and *Date* already exist in FIBO, use these classes throughout the whole ontology.

References

1. Zhou, Y., Perzylo, A.: Ontosustain: Towards an ontology for corporate sustainability reporting. In: International Semantic Web Conference (ISWC) (2023). https://www.researchgate.net/publication/375025214_OntoSustain_Towards_an_Ontology_for_Corporate_Sustainability_Reporting
2. Usmanova, A., Usbeck, R.: Structuring sustainability reports for environmental standards with LLMs guided by ontology. In: Proceedings of the 1st Workshop on Natural Language Processing Meets Climate Change (ClimateNLP 2024), pp. 168–177. Association for Computational Linguistics, August 2024. https://doi.org/10.18653/v1/2024.climatenlp-1.13

[9] https://www.spec.edmcouncil.org/fibo/ontology/LOAN/LoansGeneral/MetadataLOANLoansGeneral/LoansGeneralModule.

3. Bennett, M.: The financial industry business ontology: best practice for big data. J. Bank. Regul. **14**(3), 255–268 (2013). https://doi.org/10.1057/jbr.2013.13
4. Aidan Hogan, A., et al.: Knowledge Graphs. Synthesis Lectures on Data, Semantics, and Knowledge. Morgan & Claypool Publishers (2021)
5. Singhal, A.: Introducing the Knowledge Graph: Things, Not Strings, 5 (2012). https://blog.google/products/search/introducing-knowledge-graph-things-not/. Blog post
6. Krishnan, A.: Making search easier: How amazon's product graph is helping customers find products more easily (2018). https://www.aboutamazon.com/news/innovation-at-amazon/making-search-easier
7. Auer, S., Bizer, C., Kobilarov, G., Lehmann, J., Cyganiak, R., Ives, Z.: DBpedia: a nucleus for a web of open data. In: Aberer, K., (eds.) ASWC/ISWC -2007. LNCS, vol. 4825, pp. 722–735. Springer, Heidelberg (2007). https://doi.org/10.1007/978-3-540-76298-0_52
8. Vrandecic, D., Krötzsch, M.: Wikidata: a free collaborative knowledgebase. Commun. ACM **57**(10), 78–85 (2014). https://doi.org/10.1145/2629489
9. Suchanek, F.M., Kasneci, G., Weikum, G.: Yago: a core of semantic knowledge. In: Proceedings of the 16th International Conference on World Wide Web, WWW 2007, Banff, Alberta, Canada, May 8-12, 2007, pp. 697–706. ACM (2007). https://doi.org/10.1145/2629489
10. Angele, J., Angele, K.: Oo-logic: a successor of f-logic. In: RuleML+RR (2019). https://api.semanticscholar.org/CorpusID:203587962
11. Angele, K., Angele, J., Simsek, U., Fensel, D.: Semreasoner - a high-performance knowledge graph store and rule-based reasoner. In: The Semantic Web, pp. 574–590, Cham, 2023. Springer Nature Switzerland. https://doi.org/10.1007/978-3-031-33455-9_34
12. Pan, S., Luo, L., Wang, Y., Chen, C., Wang, J., Xindong, W.: Unifying large language models and knowledge graphs: A roadmap. IEEE Trans. Knowl. Data Eng. **36**(7), 3580–3599 (2024). https://doi.org/10.1109/TKDE.2024.3352100
13. Pan, J.Z., et al.: Large language models and knowledge graphs: Opportunities and challenges (2023). https://arxiv.org/abs/2308.06374
14. Edge, D., et al.: From local to global: a graph rag approach to query-focused summarization (2025). https://arxiv.org/abs/2404.16130
15. Weichel, H., Schäfer, J., Simon, M.: Robust table information extraction from sustainability reports: a time-aware hybrid two-step approach. In: Proceedings of the 2nd Workshop on Natural Language Processing Meets Climate Change (ClimateNLP 2025), Vienna, Austria, 2025. Association for Computational Linguistics
16. Madlberger, L., Thöni, A., Wetz, P., Schatten, A., Min Tjoa, A.: Ontology-based data integration for corporate sustainability information systems. In: Proceedings of International Conference on Information Integration and Web-Based Applications & Services, IIWAS '13, pp. 353–357, New York, NY, USA, 2013. Association for Computing Machinery. https://doi.org/10.1145/2539150.2539208
17. Yaldo, ISY.: An Ontology for Sustainability Reporting Based on Global Reporting Initiative (GRI) G4. PhD thesis (2015). https://api.semanticscholar.org/CorpusID:157531311
18. Helmke, H., Hafner, H.P., Gebert, F., Pankiewicz, A.: Provision of climate services—The XDC Model. In: Handbook of Climate Services. Cham: Springer International Publishing, 2020, pp. 223–249. https://doi.org/10.1007/978-3-030-36875-3_12

19. Passaro, R., Schumacher, B., Pellegrino, J.: Financing the transition? taking the temperature of European banks' corporate loan books. EBA Staff Paper (2024). https://www.eba.europa.eu/sites/default/files/2024-11/2e1b1d1d-3cf3-4075-a9fc-899dcf5a8460/Staff%20Paper_Financing%20the%20transition.pdf
20. Weichel, H., Zinovev, A., Haario, H., Simon, M.: Uncertainty quantification in portfolio temperature alignment (2024). https://arxiv.org/abs/2412.14182
21. Shimizu, C., Hammar, K., Hitzler, P.: Modular ontology modeling. **14**(3), 459–489 (2023). https://doi.org/10.3233/SW-222886
22. Hitzler, P., Krisnadhi, A.: A tutorial on modular ontology modeling with ontology design patterns: the cooking recipes ontology (2018). https://arxiv.org/abs/1808.08433
23. Monfardini, G.K.Q., Salamon, J.S., Barcellos, M.P.: Use of competency questions in ontology engineering: a survey. pp. 45–64, 10 (2023). https://doi.org/10.1007/978-3-031-47262-6_3
24. Jackson, R.C., Balhoff, J.P., Douglass, E., Harris, N.L., Mungall, C.J., Overton, J.A.: ROBOT: a tool for automating ontology workflows. **20**(1), 407 (2019). https://doi.org/10.1186/s12859-019-3002-3

Offline-First Strategies in Multi-cloud Environments–A Survey on the Applicability of Workload Placement in Sky Computing

Henry-Norbert Cocos(✉), Christian Baun, and Martin Kappes

Department of Computer Science and Engineering, Frankfurt University of Applied Sciences, Frankfurt am Main 60318, Germany
{cocos,christianbaun,kappes}@fra-uas.de

Abstract. This paper investigates the applicability of offline-first strategies for workload placement in multi-cloud environments, focusing on integrating on-premise resources. The authors analyze the evolution from traditional on-premise IT infrastructures to hybrid and multi-cloud models, highlighting the growing complexity of interoperability, cost management, and vendor lock-in. Sky Computing is presented as a paradigm that abstracts cloud resources across providers via an inter-cloud broker, enabling dynamic, vendor-agnostic resource allocation and service migration. The paper explores the challenges of secure connectivity, data gravity, and latency in distributed environments. It discusses the role of Software Defined Networking (SDN) and Secure Access Service Edge (SASE) in facilitating seamless and secure integration of on-premise and cloud workloads. A key contribution is introducing the SKY CONTROL framework, designed to address the specific needs of small and medium-sized enterprises (SMEs) by providing cost and risk management, infrastructure transparency, and support for geographic workload distribution. The study concludes that Sky Computing and offline-first strategies offer significant potential for enhancing flexibility and resilience in multi-cloud environments. However, further research is needed to develop standardized methodologies for workload placement and address open interoperability and security challenges.

Keywords: Offline-First-Strategy · virtualization · Sky computing · multi-cloud · vendor-agnostic framework · workload placement · resource allocation · resource provisioning · service migration

1 Introduction

Cloud Computing leverages distributed systems [34], virtualization, and modern web technologies to deliver scalable infrastructure, platforms, and applications as on-demand services. According to the National Institute of Standards and Technology (NIST), Cloud Computing is characterized by five essential properties [24]:

J. Schäfer and J. Boubeta-Puig (Eds.): SGSOACS 2025, CCIS 2831, pp. 44–58, 2026.
https://doi.org/10.1007/978-3-032-14816-2_4

- **On-demand self-service:** Automatic resource provisioning.
- **Broad network access:** Accessibility via standard network interfaces.
- **Resource pooling:** Shared, scalable resources.
- **Rapid elasticity:** Dynamic scalability.
- **Measured service:** Usage-based billing.

These features enable seamless cloud integration while lowering costs and operational effort. Figure 1 outlines the NIST model, detailing service properties, deployment types, and architectural layers.

Since the late 2000s, IT infrastructures have shifted from on-premise systems to multi-cloud and hybrid models [14,15], with multi-cloud strategies combining services across providers becoming mainstream by the mid-2010s [18]. Key advantages include vendor diversification, risk mitigation, and optimized resource allocation [13,15,30].

- Reduced provider dependency
- Cost optimization
- Load balancing
- Business continuity through redundancy
- Free service selection
- Enhanced security via data diversification

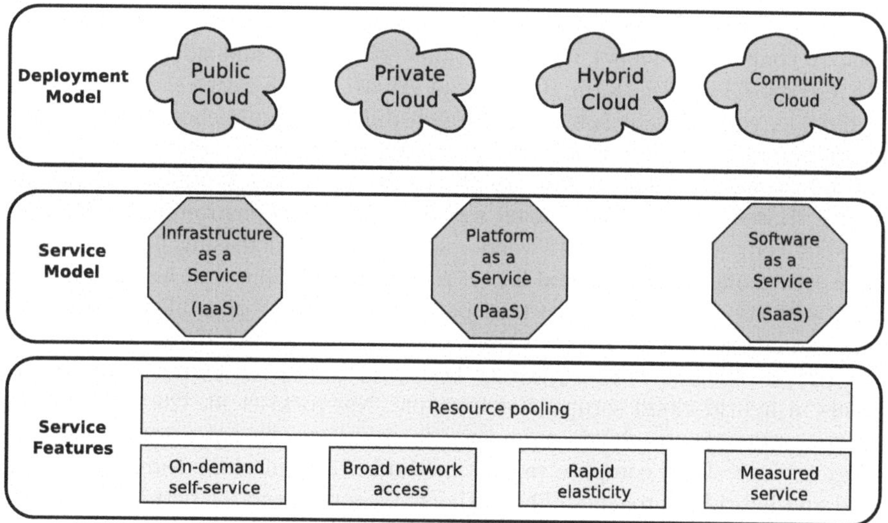

Fig. 1. NIST definition of cloud computing [8]

Multi-cloud strategies drive innovation by combining diverse platforms. At the same time, hybrid models leverage infrastructure-as-a-service (IaaS) to reduce administrative workloads and software-as-a-service (SaaS) for streamlined configuration and integration. However, managing multi-cloud systems remains complex, with interoperability posing a significant hurdle. Sky Computing addresses these issues by abstracting cloud resources across providers, allowing a dynamic selection of optimal services. Though still evolving, this approach holds considerable promise for improving multi-cloud adoption. This paper investigates Sky Computing's principles and potential to advance cloud computing paradigms.

2 Background and Related Works

Cloud computing is a model that provides computing resources such as networks, storage, and applications as services, allowing users to flexibly and cost-effectively access resources on demand. Ibrahimi [16] considers three main groups of different pricing models in cloud computing:

- Static pricing offers fixed prices regardless of demand, making it simple but less responsive to market changes.
- Dynamic pricing adjusts prices based on supply and demand in real-time, maximizing provider profit but introducing user unpredictability.
- Pay-per-use charges users only for actual consumption, while subscription models offer a fixed fee for a set period.

Choosing the right pricing model is crucial for the success of cloud services. A comparison shows the importance of fairness and adaptability, with both Google Cloud Platform (GCP) and Amazon Web Services (AWS) offering flexible, cost-efficient solutions through different approaches. However, the comparison of Ibrahimi [16] is limited to AWS and GCP.

Cloud computing has grown rapidly, resulting in varied public and private services. Based on the hybrid cloud model, multi-cloud environments are common and help companies avoid vendor lock-in while increasing flexibility [25]. These setups offer flexibility and better resource availability but also bring challenges such as a lack of service transparency, API interoperability issues, and complex management [2,4].

There is a lot of work regarding best practices for resources and pricing models in hybrid cloud setups. For example, Nawrocki et al. [26] review optimization strategies in cloud computing, focusing on efficient resource use and energy savings. They compare various methods, from machine learning to rule-based and hybrid approaches. The authors stress the need for better metrics for energy efficiency and call for more adaptive, sustainable optimization techniques. Their taxonomy helps select suitable methods and highlights the importance of combining different strategies for future research. The discussion proposes different approaches, such as statistical learning, machine learning, reinforcement learning, rule-based systems, bio-inspired algorithms, queue-based methods, and hybrid techniques that combine several strategies.

Lucanin et al. [21] introduce a pricing model where VM costs depend on allocated CPU frequency, letting users adjust performance and expenses. In their work, they develop the BCFFS (Best Cost Fit Frequency Scaling) controller, which optimizes VM distribution across geo-distributed data centers and adjusts CPU frequencies to maximize energy savings while minimizing revenue loss. Using the BCFFS controller, cloud providers can optimize VM placement and CPU frequency across data centers to save energy, achieving up to 14.57% savings while maintaining stable revenue. The approach is validated with realistic workloads and electricity price data to balance energy efficiency and profitability in dynamic cloud environments. The challenges that Lucanin et al. encountered and described were an inefficient frequency scaling scheme used in the VMs, which is especially apparent in modern multi-core systems. They emphasize the need for realistic energy models compatible with diverse architectures (Intel and ARM).

Talha et al. [23] explore whether shared cloud clusters, where multiple users pool resources to leverage cost savings through statistical multiplexing, offer substantial financial benefits compared to users renting cloud resources directly. Their work focuses explicitly on comparing pricing models for using the shared clusters. They compare a socialist approach, where costs are divided equally among users, and a capitalist approach, where Users pay based on their actual resource consumption (reserved or on-demand). However, the socialist approach can be unfair to users with lighter workloads, whereas the capitalist approach aligns costs with usage but complicates shared infrastructure management.

Software Defined Networking (SDN) is valuable for setting up virtual overlay networks. A three-layer SDN architecture [11] (infrastructure, control, management) enables centralized, dynamic resource allocation across edge and cloud nodes. This supports real-time adjustments to meet fluctuating computational demands. Even though Du et al. [11] focus on integrating edge nodes, this method is also beneficial in setting up the basis for integrating private cloud nodes into a multi-cloud setup.

Their work also analyzes different provisioning strategies, namely Lift-and-Shift, which uses reserved resources without dynamic scaling but limits flexibility. Cloud Bursting dynamically supplements reserved resources with on-demand capacity during peak demand, though this increases costs. With the Flying Solo strategy, users bypass shared clusters entirely and rent resources directly from cloud providers. One central focus point in their study was the analysis of financial incentives for using shared clusters. However, shared cloud clusters struggle to retain users due to weak financial incentives. Despite theoretical savings, the flexibility, predictability, and simplicity of direct cloud resource rental make it a choice for many, especially for bursty or latency-sensitive workloads. The paper highlights the need for better incentive structures or hybrid models to make shared clusters more appealing in practice.

The previously mentioned papers focus on pricing models and resource efficiency in cloud and multi-cloud environments but do not address interoperability between vendors and services. Stoica et al. [32,33,38] tackle this issue with Sky

Computing, a framework introducing an abstraction layer for uniform service provisioning across cloud providers [38]. The SkyPilot project [36] from Berkeley pioneers this approach with an intercloud broker optimized for machine learning workloads. However, SkyPilot is still experimental, supports limited cloud services, and focuses mainly on IaaS and machine learning workloads.

This raises questions about Sky Computing's applicability to diverse workloads and generalizability. We explore these opportunities and challenges in section 3.

3 Sky Computing

Stoica et al. [33] draw an interesting comparison between the internet and the concept of Sky Computing. The history of the internet shows how open standards and protocols like TCP/IP transformed isolated networks into a unified "network of networks." In cloud computing, a similar vision would be one where different cloud providers and services work seamlessly together. Table 1 compares the internet with Sky Computing. Their devices and terms, such as routers, form traditional networks and are mapped to servers in the cloud ecosystem. interesting in this context are the terms *Compatibility Layer* and *Intercloud Layer*, which are mapped to the *Internet Protocol* and *BGP* respectively.

The cloud landscape is fragmented, with each provider using proprietary interfaces and technologies. This makes it challenging to move data and applications between clouds. To achieve a true "Cloud of clouds," common standards and interfaces are needed that enable interoperability, just as TCP/IP did for the internet. Therefore, a means of standardized usage of resources – as the IP standard did for the internet – is needed. If such standards are widely adopted, organizations could flexibly use services from multiple clouds, avoid vendor lock-in, and improve reliability and scalability.

Table 1. Comparison between the internet and sky computing [33]

Internet	Sky computing
Router	Server
Autonomous system	Datacenter/Availability zone
Internet service provider	Cloud service provider
Enterprise network	Private cloud
Internet protocol	Compatibility layer
BGP	Intercloud layer

Sky Computing is a new concept that introduces an additional abstraction layer between cloud providers (e.g., AWS, Google Cloud) and users. With an intercloud broker, resources from different providers can be accessed seamlessly, creating a unified "cloud of clouds" [33]. The goal is to enable interoperability and decouple applications from specific cloud environments.

Sky Computing transforms cloud usage via an intercloud broker that dynamically selects providers, creating a two-sided market between users and providers. It supports multi-cloud services (e.g., Kubernetes) and cloud-specific tools (AWS Inferentia) [5]. Unlike traditional multi-cloud systems, it enables workloads to run across or split between clouds, prioritizing partial compatibility and expanding over time.

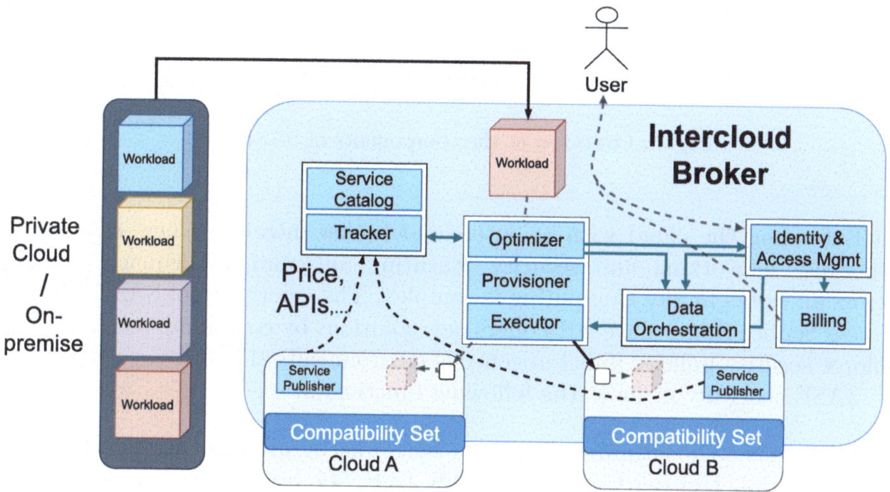

Fig. 2. Overview of the components of the inter-cloud broker [32]

Sky Computing features a distributed infrastructure that dynamically allocates workloads across providers, ensuring scalability and flexibility. Figure 2 illustrates this integrated ecosystem.

The Service Catalog lists available services, locations, APIs, and long-term prices, supporting filtering and search. The Tracker monitors frequently changing spot prices and resource availability, informing placement decisions. The Optimizer matches workloads to resources based on requirements, availability, and cost, recalculating as conditions change. The Provisioner allocates and releases resources as needed while the Executor manages workload execution. The Modules for Identity and Access Management (IAM) and Data Orchestration are directly linked to the Optimizer. The IAM module is focused on securing authorized and automated access to the workloads, which is why it also connects to the Executor. The billing module aggregates the billing information for the deployed services in the cloud. The Data Orchestration Module is responsible for managing the storage of data and the access of data by the individual services.

A key aspect is compatibility sets, which leverage existing APIs and services from all providers to enable standardized, transparent integration.

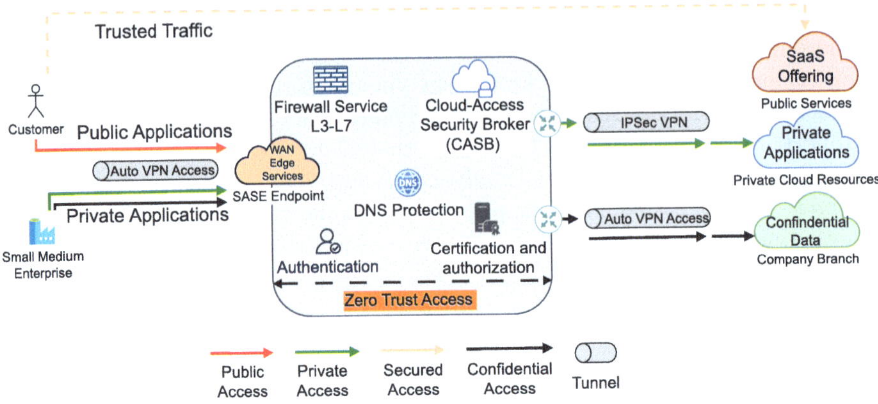

Fig. 3. Overview of the components of SASE [38]

Extending the cloud with an intercloud broker introduces new challenges, especially networking and security. Ensuring automated, adequate security across all assets in Sky Computing is complex. The emergence of SASE (Secure Access Service Edge) since 2019 offers new solutions by combining techniques to enforce security policies in heterogeneous environments [17,22].

SASE generally includes the following functionalities:

- **SD-WAN** [37] optimizes wide-area networks by allowing organizations to use multiple transport services (MPLS, LTE, 5G, broadband) for secure connectivity [17].
- **Secure Web Gateway (SWG)** filters and monitors web traffic to protect users from threats and ensure compliance.
- **Cloud Access Security Broker (CASB)** enforces security policies between cloud users and providers.
- **Firewall-as-a-Service (FWaaS)** provides scalable, cloud-based firewall functionalities.
- **Zero Trust Network Access (ZTNA)** follows the *never trust, always verify* principle, securing user sessions inside and outside corporate networks.

SASE enables centralized policy management with distributed enforcement, allowing local security decisions via CPE or device agents [35]. Integrating SASE into Sky Computing helps manage assets and risks, though practical implementation is still developing. While promising for workload distribution and interoperability, adoption, especially by SMEs, needs more research (see Sect. 5). The next section examines on-prem workload integration, followed by an approach for SMEs.

4 Offline-First-Strategies in Mulit-cloud Computing

This research topic integrates workloads into Sky Computing, geographically distributing them across WANs to develop an intercloud broker. An offline-first approach prioritizes local execution but allows cloud migration, boosting service availability and flexibility.

Offloading cloud services to client-side endpoints and selecting services for the offloading seems promising especially for SMEs, since applications reside on-prem and cooperation with the cloud is a beneficial approach. To achieve this and the conditions for the relocation should be investigated. Unlike cloud-first, an offline-first approach prioritizes local service availability, ensuring network independence while leveraging cloud collaboration for enhanced functionality.

A critical aspect is the scaling of services:

- Vertical scaling (adding resources)
- Horizontal scaling (adding service instances)
- Geographical scaling (placing services closer to users or "scaling away").

As Table 1 in Sect. 3 already demonstrated, we can map existing methods and devices from networking to the Sky Computing ecosystem. The part that is especially interesting in this line of work is the part of private clouds mapped to enterprise networks in Table 1. Here, it is essential to find technologies and methods that resemble the free flow of packets in the networking stack, so an offline-first strategy could help companies form dynamic private clouds that interact with public clouds seamlessly. Therefore, this section explores and proposes technologies, methods, and architectures that align with the Sky Computing paradigm.

Software Defined Networking (SDN) is valuable framework for setting up virtual overlay networks in the relocation of workloads (see Sect. 2). It enables centralized, dynamic resource allocation across edge and cloud nodes. This supports real-time adjustments to meet fluctuating computational demands. This setup seems to be promising in constructing a suitable foundation for the relocation of workloads.

However, an overlooked issue is the secure attachment of on-premise services to remote cloud services without manual intervention. One possible solution for this issue lies in SASE. The centralized policy management with distributed enforcement points can be beneficial in ensuring local decision-making and configuration of security and encryption methods and enforcing them via managed device agents [35].

Using the Sky Computing paradigm, an inter-cloud broker could facilitate seamless interoperability between cloud and on-premise environments. This would allow users to access nearby services independently of the cloud, increasing autonomy and resilience without losing cloud benefits.

Key objectives include:

- Defining criteria for outsourcing computing-intensive tasks, an area with no standardized research methodology.

- Investigating service migration to optimize resource distribution across cloud, end devices, and services.
- Exploring vertical migration (between cloud and end devices) and horizontal migration (between end devices), assessing their impact and technical feasibility.

A central issue in this investigation is the problem of data gravity [32]. Data gravity describes the necessity of applications needing to run near their data due to high latency and egress costs. Egress, meaning the cost of data transmission out of the cloud, remains a critical barrier to multi-cloud adoption. Another key issue is the data transfer latency between clouds, especially private clouds, due to the physical distance and network inefficiencies. Proposed solutions include network optimization, like overlay routing to provide indirect paths, and transmission engineering and structured data optimizations, like copy-on-access, where only requested records are transferred, minimizing bulk transfers, as well as caching strategies like write-through/write-back caching and prefetching, which balance cost and latency for read/write-heavy workloads.

4.1 Methods for Workload Optimization

In the literature [26], different techniques are used to optimize cloud resource usage. These methods are especially beneficial in multi-cloud environments since end users can leverage the possibilities of different services operated by different CSPs. The possible areas of optimization are the following:

- **Autoscaling:** Dynamic adjustment of resources based on demand.
- **Resource allocation:** Efficient distribution of resources to applications and users.
- **Load balancing:** Balanced distribution of workloads across available resources.
- **Virtual machine consolidation (VMC):** The number of active servers is reduced through efficient VM management.
- **Virtual machine placement (VMP):** Strategic allocation of virtual machines to physical servers based on resource availability and performance requirements.
- **Task scheduling:** Planning the execution sequence of tasks to optimize resource consumption and energy efficiency.
- **Task offloading:** Decision-making processes for offloading tasks to edge or cloud servers.
- **Resource planning and reservation:** Predicting and managing resource requirements to reduce waste.

However, only three options—VMP, task scheduling, and task offloading—are useful for optimizing workload placement in hybrid cloud setups. These strategies use offline first, since the other optimization strategies can only be applied in the cloud and do not consider on-premise workloads. VMC and VMP can be used for optimizing legacy systems of SMEs by relocating the applications to different locations. Task scheduling and Task offloading can only be used by adapting the applications and therefore heavily refactoring the applications. The SKY CONTROL framework, developed with Systrade at the Frankfurt University of Applied Sciences, is an interesting project to integrate on-prem private clouds for SMEs into the Sky Computing ecosystem. The details are explained in the following section.

5 SKY CONTROL

Multi-cloud environments offer SMEs benefits but pose challenges like workload management across CSPs, cost visibility, and security risks. SKY CONTROL tackles these issues, streamlining multi-cloud deployments. The following sections outline its architecture and functionalities tailored to SME needs.

5.1 Architecture of SKY CONTROL

As an outlook, we present the conceptual frameworks to address the challenges discussed above. SKY CONTROL [8] enables SMEs to control and optimize multi-cloud setups, easing the transition to Sky Computing. We also analyze methods for integrating workloads into the Sky Computing ecosystem, focusing on geographic distribution across WANs to inform intercloud broker implementation.

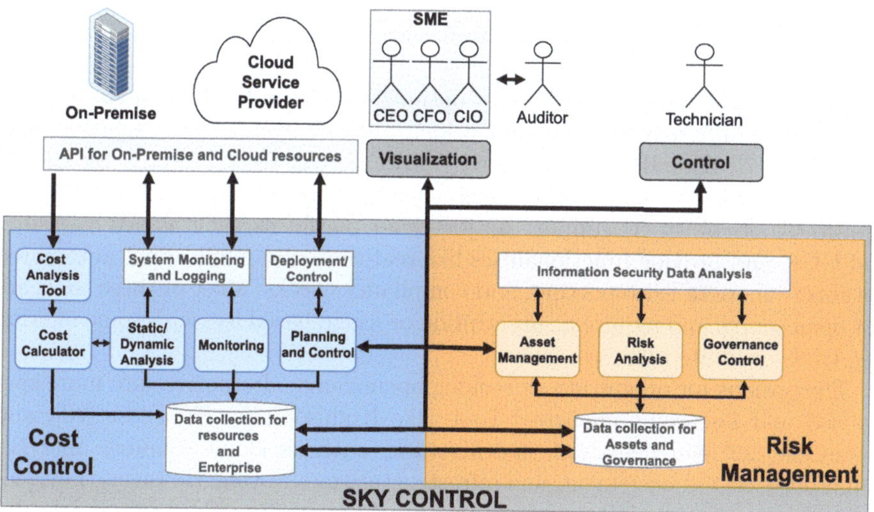

Fig. 4. SKY CONTROL architecture [8]

This section describes the key components of the SKY CONTROL framework:

- **Cost Control:** Analyzes and visualizes costs for on-prem/cloud resources via static analysis of items such as Resource IDs and hardware specs and dynamic analysis of CPU/memory usage and network bandwidth to generate pricing trends/predictions, accounting for cloud integration complexity. It includes a control/planning tool with multi-cloud usage insights and visualizations.
- **Risk Management:** Manages assets, analyzes risks (asset criticality, data sensitivity, compliance with standards like C5 [10]), and ensures compliance for German SMEs. Enhances enterprise compatibility and provides risk/asset visualization for CIOs, streamlining audits and mitigation.

Figure 4 illustrates the architecture of the proposed framework.

5.2 Cost Control and Securing Access

Managing multi-cloud costs involves infrastructure (compute, storage, networking), data transfer fees (especially between providers), and expenses for security, compliance, and vendor-specific services. Hidden costs can result from idle resources, overprovisioning, or overlapping services. Proactive monitoring and optimization are essential to prevent inefficiencies.

Cloud cost management tools offer real-time monitoring, analysis, and optimization of infrastructure expenses across major providers like AWS, Google Cloud, and Azure. They provide centralized dashboards, automated recommendations, and detailed cost breakdowns by team or project. However, most solutions are proprietary and expensive to license, making them costly for organizations.

Various tools are available for cost optimization in multi-cloud environments, each offering different features and pricing models. Commercial solutions like CloudZero [7], CloudHealth (formerly VMware Aria Cost Powered by CloudHealth) [6], Flexera One [28], Densify [9], Spot by NetApp [12], nOps [27], Apptio Cloudability [1] support major cloud platforms such as AWS, Azure, and GCP, and provide functionalities like real-time cost monitoring, automated optimization, detailed reporting, and compliance checks. Most of these tools are not open source and require a subscription or usage-based fee, with some offering free trials or limited free versions.

The options for organizations seeking open-source alternatives are more specialized and less comprehensive. Tools like Komiser [19], Kubecost [20], and OpenCost [29] can help with specific tasks such as cloud resource analysis, Kubernetes cost management, and infrastructure monitoring. However, they generally do not offer the full range of enterprise features found in commercial solutions, especially for complex, multi-cloud cost management and optimization.

These APIs are mainly used by cloud cost monitoring and optimization (CCMO) tools, which simplify cloud monitoring by operating independently of any specific cloud provider. AWS, for example, offers the AWS Billing and Cost

Management API [31], which makes it possible to inspect and extract detailed pricing information of the provided services of their service catalog. Another example is the Microsoft Cost Management API by Microsoft [3]. However, integrating this information is a complex task since the data needs to align to a standardized format and be mapped to the services used in real-time. Constructing a suitable taxonomy for resources, services, and their respective prices is an ongoing task.

This section emphasizes analyzing pricing, workload criticality, and governance to define decision criteria for workload placement. An algorithm must formalize these decisions in the Optimizer (Sect. 3). Since "optimality" depends on context, SKY CONTROL establishes a framework for evaluating criteria before integrating them into optimization.

Overall, the frameworks mentioned above all consider pricing optimization for the major cloud platforms. Still, these frameworks do not consider risk management tasks like the analysis of assets or the integration of automated provisioning tasks for automated workload placement. The only framework currently integrating these tasks is SkyPilot, developed by Berkley University [32,33]. However, this framework focuses on setting up machine learning (ML) pipelines and optimizing pricing for model training by leveraging spot instances for the training. Therefore, SKY CONTROL aims to provide complete infrastructure transparency and is designed for SMEs to be highly adaptable by integrating ML pipelines and all workloads. It leverages existing and emerging technologies to achieve this goal, some of which will inspire or be directly integrated into its architecture.

Eventhough SkyPilot is a first real world implementation of the Sky Computing paradigm it is lacking an integration of SASE. Therefore we plan to integrate this technology for the seamless access of users to workloads and services. Therefore an examination of the technological maturity and practical applicability of SASE is conducted by first compiling a sample of key providers based on publicly available information and then looking at free and open source software. The analysis focuses on the potential of SASE products for the use in hybrid multi-cloud infrastructures. SASE products should help to manage local and/or hosted infrastructures via a solutions. The solutions should also offer interfaces to the most important cloud platforms (AWS, Azure, Google) and in addition should have functionalities that focus on automation and integration. We plan to integrate these feature into SKY CONTROL making it a unified center for multi-cloud infrastructures.

However, there are still various challenges for SMEs implementing the aforementioned methods. One major problem is the cloud adoption of legacy systems. These old systems usually rely on old middleware and frameworks and use outdated interfaces between components. One way to deal with this challenge is to use the Lift-and-Shift migration method, where the workload is transferred to a virtual environment, and the application's core is not altered. This comes with drawbacks since benefits that cloud operation offers (like Autoscaling) cannot be entirely leveraged

6 Conclusion and Outlook

Sky Computing simplifies multi-cloud management by abstracting vendor APIs via an inter-cloud broker. Our analysis identifies implementation challenges, highlighting the need for new frameworks and tools to create a user-centric marketplace.

SKY CONTROL provides tailored cost/risk management for SMEs through dynamic analysis, real-time cost tracking, and risk assessment, enhancing infrastructure transparency. Its Sky Computing integration boosts multi-cloud efficiency, offering SMEs competitive flexibility. However, the project is still in its infancy and, therefore, still a largely conceptual work in progress. Thus, many open problems need to be tackled. One would be the organizational challenges of implementing Sky Computing in practice for SMEs while fulfilling compliance standards and ensuring security over multiple cloud vendors. The different APIs, locations of data centers, and overall heterogeneous nature of the CSP service offerings make it very challenging to implement this in practice.

We explored geographic workload distribution across WANs and an offline-first strategy for local/cloud flexibility. While this concept paper outlines foundational ideas, many questions remain open. Future work aims to deliver actionable solutions.

Acknowledgments. The SKY CONTROL project described in this paper is funded by the *"Federal Ministry for Economic Affairs and Climate Action ('Bundesministerium für Wirtschaft und Klimaschutz')"* in the framework of the central innovation programme for small and medium-sized enterprises ('Zentrales Innovationsprogramm Mittelstand'), at Frankfurt University of Applied Sciences and is realized in cooperation with the company Systrade GmbH.

References

1. Apptio: IBM Cloudability. https://www.apptio.com/products/cloudability/
2. Ardagna, D.: Cloud and multi-cloud computing: Current challenges and future applications. In: 2015 IEEE/ACM 7th International Workshop on Principles of Engineering Service-Oriented and Cloud Systems, pp. 1–2 (2015). https://doi.org/10.1109/PESOS.2015.8
3. Azure, M.: Microsoft cost management. http://learn.microsoft.com/en-us/rest/api/cost-management/
4. Barker, A., Varghese, B., Thai, L.: Cloud services brokerage: a survey and research roadmap. In: 2015 IEEE 8th International Conference on Cloud Computing, pp. 1029–1032 (2015). https://doi.org/10.1109/CLOUD.2015.144
5. Chasins, S., Cheung, A., Crooks, N., Ghodsi, A., Goldberg, K., Gonzalez, J.E., Hellerstein, J.M., Jordan, M.I., Joseph, A.D., Mahoney, M.W., Parameswaran, A., Patterson, D., Popa, R.A., Sen, K., Shenker, S., Song, D., Stoica, I.: The sky above the clouds (2022). arXiv:2205.07147
6. CloudHealth: Continuous cloud cost optimization. https://www.vmware.com/products/app-platform/tanzu-cloudhealth

7. CloudZero: Cloud Cost Visibility and Savings. https://www.cloudzero.com/
8. Cocos, H., Baun, C., Kappes, M.: The evolution of cloud computing towards a vendor agnostic market place using the SKY CONTROL framework. In: Proceedings of the 15th International Conference on Cloud Computing and Services Science - CLOSER, pp. 211–218. INSTICC, SciTePress (2025). https://doi.org/10.5220/0013361200003950
9. Densify: Automated Kubernetes Optimization. https://www.densify.com/
10. Di Giulio, C., Sprabery, R., Kamhoua, C., Kwiat, K., Campbell, R.H., Bashir, M.N.: Cloud standards in comparison: are new security frameworks improving cloud security? In: 2017 IEEE 10th International Conference on Cloud Computing (CLOUD), pp. 50–57 (2017). https://doi.org/10.1109/CLOUD.2017.16
11. Du, J., Jiang, C., Benslimane, A., Guo, S., Ren, Y.: SDN-based resource allocation in edge and cloud computing systems: an evolutionary Stackelberg differential game approach. IEEE ACM Trans. Netw. **30**(4), 1613–1628 (2022)
12. by Flexera, S.: Control costs, Optimize infrastructure, Elevate cloud performance. https://spot.io/
13. Georgios, C., Evangelia, F., Christos, M., Maria, N.: Exploring cost-efficient bundling in a multi-cloud environment. Simul. Model. Pract. Theory **111**, 102338 (2021). https://doi.org/10.1016/j.simpat.2021.102338, https://www.sciencedirect.com/science/article/pii/S1569190X2100054X
14. Gundu, S.R., Panem, C.A., Thimmapuram, A.: Hybrid it and multi cloud an emerging trend and improved performance in cloud computing. SN Comput. Sci. **1**(5) (2020). https://doi.org/10.1007/s42979-020-00277-x
15. Hong, J., Dreibholz, T., Schenkel, J.A., Hu, J.A.: An Overview of Multi-cloud Computing. In: Barolli, L., Takizawa, M., Xhafa, F., Enokido, T. (eds.) WAINA 2019. AISC, vol. 927, pp. 1055–1068. Springer, Cham (2019). https://doi.org/10.1007/978-3-030-15035-8_103
16. Ibrahimi, A.: Cloud computing: pricing model. Int. J. Adv. Comput. Sci. Appl. **8**(6) (2017). https://doi.org/10.14569/IJACSA.2017.080658
17. Islam, M.N., Colomo-Palacios, R., Chockalingam, S.: Secure access service edge: a multivocal literature review. In: 2021 21st International Conference on Computational Science and Its Applications (ICCSA), pp. 188–194 (2021). https://doi.org/10.1109/ICCSA54496.2021.00034
18. Jamshidi, P., Pahl, C., Mendonça, N.C.: Pattern-based multi-cloud architecture migration. Softw.: Pract. Exp. **47**(9), 1159–1184 (2016). https://doi.org/10.1002/spe.2442
19. Komiser: GitHub Repository. https://github.com/tailwarden/komiser
20. kubecost: Monitor and reduce Kubernetes spend. https://www.kubecost.com/
21. Lucanin, D., Pietri, I., Holmbacka, S., Brandic, I., Lilius, J., Sakellariou, R.: Performance-based pricing in multi-core geo-distributed cloud computing. IEEE Trans. Cloud Comput. **8**(4), 1079–1092 (2020)
22. MacDonald, N., Orans, L., Skorupa, J.: The future of network security is in the cloud. Gartner (2019)
23. Mehboob, T., Bashir, N., Zink, M., Irwin, D.: Is sharing caring? analyzing the incentives for shared cloud clusters. In: Proceedings of the 2023 ACM/SPEC International Conference on Performance Engineering, pp. 7–16. ICPE '23, Association for Computing Machinery, New York, NY, USA (2023). https://doi.org/10.1145/3578244.3583730
24. Mell, P., Grance, T., of Standards, N.I., Division, T.U.C.S.: The NIST Definition of Cloud Computing. NIST special publication, U.S. Department of Commerce,

National Institute of Standards and Technology (2011). https://books.google.es/books?id=WyHhAQAACAAJ
25. Mulder, J.: Multi-cloud architecture and governance: leverage azure, AWS, GCP, and VMware vSphere to build effective multi-cloud solutions. Packt Publishing (2020). https://books.google.es/books?id=ZjgKEAAAQBAJ
26. Nawrocki, P., Smendowski, M.: A survey of cloud resource consumption optimization methods. J. Grid Comput. **23**(1) (2025)
27. nOps: Use less cloud, and pay less for what you use. https://www.nops.io/
28. One, F.: Optimize your IT with full visibility, cost control and compliance. https://www.flexera.com/products/flexera-one
29. OpenCost: Open source cost monitoring for cloud native environments. https://opencost.io/
30. Petcu, D.: Multi-cloud: expectations and current approaches. In: Proceedings of the 2013 International Workshop on Multi-cloud Applications and Federated Clouds. ICPE'13, ACM (2013). https://doi.org/10.1145/2462326.2462328
31. Services, A.W.: What is AWS billing and cost management? https://docs.aws.amazon.com/awsaccountbilling/latest/aboutv2/billing-what-is.html
32. Stoica, I.: Sky computing: opportunities and challenges. In: Studies in Systems, Decision and Control. Studies in Systems, Decision and Control, pp. 15–27. Springer Nature Switzerland, Cham (2024)
33. Stoica, I., Shenker, S.: From cloud computing to sky computing. In: Proceedings of the Workshop on Hot Topics in Operating Systems, pp. 26–32. HotOS '21, ACM, New York, NY, USA (2021). https://doi.org/10.1145/3458336.3465301
34. van Steen, M., Tanenbaum, A.: Distributed Systems. Maarten van Steen, 3rd edn. (2017), self-published, open publication
35. van der Walt, S., Venter, H.: Research gaps and opportunities for secure access service edge. In: International Conference on Cyber Warfare and Security, pp. 609–619 (2022)
36. Wei, X., Mohaimenur Rahman, A.B.M., Wang, Y.: Data placement strategies for data-intensive computing over edge clouds. In: 2021 IEEE International Performance, Computing, and Communications Conference (IPCCC), pp. 1–8 (2021). https://doi.org/10.1109/IPCCC51483.2021.9679438
37. Yang, Z., Cui, Y., Li, B., Liu, Y., Xu, Y.: Software-defined wide area network (SD-WAN): architecture, advances and opportunities. In: 2019 28th International Conference on Computer Communication and Networks (ICCCN), pp. 1–9 (2019). https://doi.org/10.1109/ICCCN.2019.8847124
38. Yang, Z., Wu, Z., Luo, M., Chiang, W.L., Bhardwaj, R., Kwon, W., Zhuang, S., Luan, F.S., Mittal, G., Shenker, S., Stoica, I.: SkyPilot: An intercloud broker for sky computing. In: 20th USENIX Symposium on Networked Systems Design and Implementation (NSDI 23), pp. 437–455. USENIX Association, Boston, MA (2023). https://www.usenix.org/conference/nsdi23/presentation/yang-zongheng

Interactive Exploration of Concept Lattices with lattice.js: A Web-Based Visualization Library

Fabiola Hodo[1,2(✉)], Sara Balderas-Díaz[2], Gabriel Guerrero-Contreras[2], and Barış Sertkaya[1]

[1] Computer Science and Engineering, Frankfurt University of Applied Sciences, 60318 Frankfurt am Main, Germany
{fabiola.hodo,sertkaya}@fra-uas.de

[2] Department of Computer Science and Engineering, University of Cadiz, Av. Universidad de Cádiz, 10, Puerto Real, 11519 Cádiz, Spain
{sara.balderas,gabriel.guerrero}@uca.es

Abstract. Concept lattices are central to Formal Concept Analysis (FCA), offering a structured and interpretable way to represent and analyze relationships between objects and attributes. However, producing clear and interactive lattice visualizations remains challenging, especially for larger or more complex datasets. Existing FCA tools often lack interactive features or rely on outdated technologies, limiting their accessibility and usability. In this paper, we introduce `lattice.js`, a lightweight JavaScript library designed for the interactive visualization of concept lattices. Built on top of the D3.js framework, `lattice.js` supports hierarchical layout computation using a heuristic adaptation of the Coffman–Graham algorithm combined with barycentric reordering to improve readability. The library also offers interactive exploration features such as zooming, filtering, node selection, and reduced labeling strategies. Additionally, it provides structural metric computation and supports exporting visualizations in multiple formats. We demonstrate the library's functionality using a well-known FCA example, highlighting its accessibility and practical value for FCA applications.

Keywords: FCA · Concept Lattice · Interactive Visualization

1 Introduction

Formal Concept Analysis (FCA) is a mathematical framework for knowledge representation, data analysis, and information management. Originating from lattice theory as introduced by Rudolf Wille in the early 1980s [13], FCA structures data into formal contexts and derives conceptual hierarchies known as concept lattices. These lattices serve as interpretable models for exploring the relationships between objects and their attributes. Visualizing such lattices plays a crucial role in supporting human understanding and knowledge discovery.

J. Schäfer and J. Boubeta-Puig (Eds.): SGSOACS 2025, CCIS 2831, pp. 59–70, 2026.
https://doi.org/10.1007/978-3-032-14816-2_5

However, designing clear and informative concept lattice visualizations becomes increasingly difficult as the size and complexity of the lattice grow. According to Eades et al. [11] and Freese [12], effective graph drawing should clearly illustrate the hierarchical structure, distribute nodes evenly, and minimize edge crossings to reduce visual clutter.

Over the years, several open-source FCA tools have been developed. The website of Uta Priss[1] gives a clear and detailed look at the history of the field. Wille [25] pointed out how important concept lattices are and highlighted how useful visualizations can be in supporting data understanding.

Early tools like ConExp [26], ToscanaJ [3], and Galicia [23] became widely used to compute and explore lattices. FCAStone [21] focused on file interoperability, while Lattice Miner [4,19] supported pattern querying and approximation. OpenFCA [6] introduced a full suite for editing and visualization. Conexp-clj [5,16] remains active, with extensions such as DimDraw [10] built in Clojure.

However, many of these tools are no longer actively maintained. Those that remain often depend on specialized languages or lack integration flexibility. Conexp-clj, for instance, requires familiarity with Clojure, which can present a barrier to adoption for users unfamiliar with that language.

Efforts such as Visualizing Formal Concept Trees [2] and LatViz [1] introduced web-based solutions. Although LatViz remains functional, its interactivity is limited and it lacks extensibility to support integration with other tools.

A more recent development is FCA4J [15], a Java library that provides comprehensive functionality for both FCA and Relational Concept Analysis(RCA). Although FCA4J excels in algorithmic functionality and supports use cases such as implication exploration and data cleaning, it lacks a built-in visualization module and relies on external tools such as RCAviz [20] for visual exploration. However, RCAviz is primarily designed to navigate relational concept structures in RCA. It does not offer rich interactivity, such as concept filtering, dynamic relabeling, or user-driven manipulation of the layout, making it less suited for detailed exploration of standard FCA lattices.

To address these limitations, we introduce `lattice.js`[2], an open-source JavaScript library for interactive and scalable concept lattice visualization. Built on top of the D3.js framework [7], `lattice.js` supports hierarchical layering, customizable labeling, interactive filtering, structural metric computation, multi-format export. Unlike platform-specific or static FCA tools, it is modular, developer-friendly, and well-suited for integration into modern FCA workflows in both research and educational contexts. In addition to describing the interface and functionalities, this paper explains the layout algorithms used in the visualizations. In particular, `lattice.js` applies a heuristic variant of the Coffman–Graham algorithm combined with barycentric reordering to produce layered lattice layouts with minimal edge crossings.

This paper is an extended version of a preliminary work presented at the Fifth Doctoral Consortium in Computer Science at the University of Cádiz (JIPII

[1] https://upriss.github.io/fca/fca.html.
[2] https://github.com/fabiolahodo/lattice.

2025) [18]. In this extended version, we provide a refined discussion of the layering algorithms and introduce new features, including shortest path computation and extended export functionality. While the previous version only supported exporting the concept lattice, the current version also allows exporting the reconstructed formal context in both CSV and CXT formats.

The remainder of this paper is structured as follows. Section 2 provides the theoretical foundations of Formal Concept Analysis (FCA) relevant to our visualization approach. Section 3 describes the layout and rendering methodology implemented in `lattice.js`, focusing on layering strategies and edge crossing minimization. Section 4 presents the key features and interactive functionalities supported by the library. Section 5 discusses the current limitations and outlines directions for future development. Finally, Sect. 6 summarizes our contributions and highlights the role of `lattice.js` in the advancement of interactive concept lattice visualization.

2 Background

To ensure this paper is self-contained, we begin by reviewing the fundamental concepts of FCA, including formal contexts, formal concepts, and concept lattices, based primarily on the work of Ganter and Wille [13]. In the second part of this section, we introduce key graph-drawing techniques relevant to visualizing concept lattices, with a focus on hierarchical layout algorithms. Specifically, we discuss the Coffman–Graham layering algorithm [9] and the barycenter heuristic [22], which together support the generation of readable and structurally faithful concept lattice layouts.

Definition 1 (Formal Context). *A triple (G, M, I) is called a* formal context *if G and M are sets, and $I \subseteq G \times M$ is a binary relation between G and M. Typically, the elements of G are referred to as* objects, *and the elements of M as* attributes.

Table 1 illustrates a simple formal context related to gender and age. Rows represent objects (e.g., *girl*, *man*) and columns represent attributes (e.g., *juvenile*, *male*). A 'x' indicates that a particular object has a given attribute.

Table 1. A formal context with gender and age attributes

	Female	Juvenile	Adult	Male
Girl	×	×		
Woman	×		×	
Boy		×		×
Man			×	×

We will refer to the formal context using the notation (G, M, I). Having established this foundational structure, we now proceed to define the notion of a formal concept.

Definition 2 (Formal Concept). *A* formal concept *of* (G, M, I) *is a pair of sets* (A, B)*, where* $A \subseteq G$ *and* $B \subseteq M$*, satisfying the conditions* $A' = B$ *and* $B' = A$*. In this context:*

- *A, known as the* extent*, represents a subset of objects;*
- *B, the* intent*, represents a subset of attributes.*

The extent and intent are related such that every object in the extent has every attribute in the intent, and every attribute in the intent applies to every object in the extent.

The set of all formal concepts of a context naturally forms a partially ordered set, known as a *concept lattice*, defined as follows:

Definition 3 (Concept Lattice). *The* concept lattice *of a formal context* (G, M, I)*, denoted as* $\mathcal{B}(G, M, I)$*, is the set of all formal concepts ordered by the* subconcept–superconcept *relation:*

The concepts in $\mathcal{B}(G, M, I)$ *are ordered by the* subconcept-superconcept *relation:*

$$(A_1, B_1) \leq (A_2, B_2) \quad \textit{if and only if} \quad A_1 \subseteq A_2 \quad (\textit{equivalently, } B_2 \supseteq B_1).$$

This order induces a lattice structure that captures the hierarchical relationships among concepts.

Figure 1 shows the concept lattice derived from the formal context in Table 1. Each node in the lattice corresponds to a formal concept, consisting of an extent

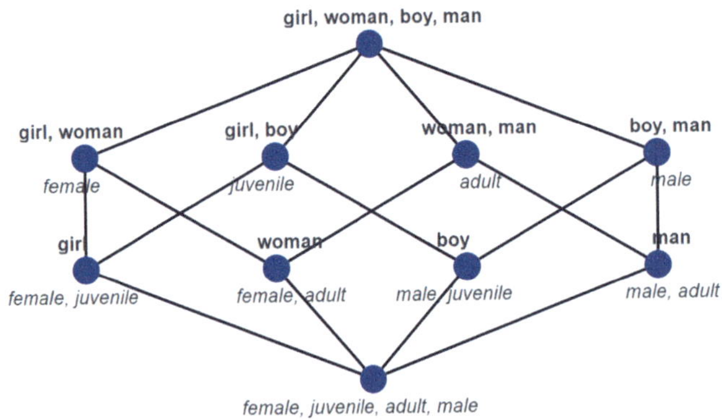

Fig. 1. Concept lattice constructed from the formal context in Table 1. The nodes are labeled with extents (in bold, representing object names such as **girl or woman**) and intents (in italics, representing attributes such as *female or adult*).

(in bold) and intent (in italics), which together illustrate the relationship between objects and attributes. The lattice structure reflects a partial order, where edges indicate subconcept–superconcept relationships.

To compute layered layouts of concept lattices for visualization, `lattice.js` applies established techniques from hierarchical graph drawing. The two main methods used are Coffman–Graham layering algorithm and the barycenter heuristic. The Coffman–Graham algorithm assigns nodes to layers while respecting width constraints. The barycenter heuristic is applied during the vertex ordering phase to reduce edge crossings between adjacent layers—a problem that is NP-hard even in the two-layer case [11,14]. These methods are defined below.

Definition 4 (Coffman–Graham Layering). *The Coffman–Graham algorithm computes a layering of a DAG* $G = (V, E)$*, placing nodes into layers* $L_0, L_1, \ldots, L_h$*, such that:*

- *Edges flow from lower to higher layers (i.e.,* $(u, v) \in E \Rightarrow \ell(u) < \ell(v)$*),*
- *Each layer* L_i *contains at most* W *nodes (width constraint),*
- *The number of layers* h *is minimized.*

This method is commonly used in hierarchical graph drawing and scheduling problems where structural constraints must be preserved while balancing height and width.

Definition 5 (Barycenter Heuristic). *The* barycenter heuristic *places each vertex at the average horizontal position of its neighbors in the adjacent layer. This method is commonly used to order vertices in hierarchical layouts to reduce edge crossings. While it does not guarantee optimality, it is fast and typically produces high-quality orderings.*

These theoretical foundations guide the design and implementation of *lattice.js*, which integrates them into an interactive visualization framework. The following section outlines the library's key features and design choices.

3 Method

The layout generation in `lattice.js` builds on established methods for the hierarchical visualization of concept lattices. In particular, it leverages the Coffman–Graham algorithm [9] for assigning formal concepts to hierarchical layers. Originally developed for scheduling problems, the Coffman–Graham algorithm has since been adapted for hierarchical graph drawing [17].

The classical Coffman–Graham algorithm typically requires preprocessing steps such as topological sorting and often introduces dummy vertexes to handle long edges spanning multiple layers. In the context of FCA, introducing such dummy concepts may obscure the interpretability of the lattice by altering the original conceptual structure.

To address this limitation, `lattice.js` implements a heuristic variant of Coffman–Graham specifically tailored to concept lattices. Our approach avoids the introduction of dummy concepts, thereby preserving the integrity, reserving the original structure and improving interpretability, of the lattice structure. Layer spacing is heuristically determined based on the overall lattice size and the number of concepts per layer, resulting in balanced and readable layouts suitable for interactive exploration.

For ordering nodes within each layer, we apply the barycenter heuristic [22] to minimize edge crossings between subconcept–superconcept relationships, it positions each node based on the average horizontal position of its neighbors in adjacent layers. Although minimizing edge crossings between layers is an NP-hard problem [11,14], the barycenter heuristic offers a practical trade-off: it runs efficiently and typically achieves near-optimal layouts in empirical evaluations [8]. In `lattice.js`, this is achieved through a multi-pass reordering strategy, alternating between top-down and bottom-up passes, to improve the horizontal alignment of related concepts.

To further refine the layout, `lattice.js` performs post-processing steps such as midpoint straightening to align nearly linear chains of concepts, and edge disambiguation to improve visual clarity and minimize overlap. These refinements, combined with earlier layering strategies, result in scalable and readable concept lattice visualizations that support real-time interaction. Additionally, lattice.js transforms serialized data into graph structures, computes both reduced and full labels, and renders the lattice using scalable vector graphics (SVG). Core interactive features and structural analysis capabilities—such as zooming, node selection, metric computation, and formal context construction—are supported and further detailed in the following section.

4 Key Features and Functionalities

`lattice.js` implements algorithmic and interactive features designed to advance the visualization and exploration of concept lattices in FCA. Building on techniques such as Coffman–Graham layering and barycentric reordering, the library supports the construction of hierarchical lattice structures that minimize edge crossings and reduce visual clutter. In addition to layout optimization, `lattice.js` provides interactive exploration features, labeling strategies (including reduced labeling based on propagation algorithms), structural metrics computation, and file handling utilities. Together, these features make `lattice.js` a flexible and extensible research tool for investigating layout algorithms, enabling intuitive user interaction, and supporting the knowledge representation within the FCA framework.

4.1 Layering Strategies

`lattice.js` supports two strategies for assigning formal concepts into hierarchical layers, depending on the nature of the input data:

Predefined 'level': When the input data provides predefined levels, the library directly uses these to organize the concepts. This approach allows for user-defined structuring and supports integration with external lattice generators that compute levels in advance.

Coffman-Graham Algorithm: In the absence of level values, it applies a heuristic variant of the Coffman-Graham algorithm to dynamically compute layers while preserving subconcept-superconcept relationships. Additional heuristics adjust layer spacing and optimize node positioning to enhance readability.

4.2 Interactive Exploration

Understanding concept lattices can be challenging without the ability to interact with them. To make this process more intuitive and engaging, the library enables users to interact with the concept lattice through several features:

- **Zooming:** Users can zoom in and out of the lattice to explore details or gain an overview using the mouse wheel or touchpad gestures on the laptop. Additionally, zooming is automatically activated when a user clicks on a node, causing the view to focus on the selected concept and scale appropriately.
- **Node Dragging:** Concepts can be repositioned horizontally while maintaining their vertical alignment to preserve the lattice hierarchy. A node cannot be moved above its superconcepts or below its subconcepts. This design provides a balance between interactivity and structural integrity, allowing users to customize the layout while respecting the underlying concept relationships.
- **Node Selection:** Clicking on a concept highlights its position and displays additional information such as its ID, label, extent and intent sizes, stability and neighborhood size.
- **Tooltips:** Hovering over a concept displays essential information such as the concept ID, label, and level, offering immediate context without interrupting the flow of exploration.
- **Filtering:** To help users focus on relevant parts of the lattice, lattice.js includes a filtering mechanism that allows concepts to be highlighted based on objects or attributes. Users can input one or more object or attribute names, and the visualization will dynamically update to show which concepts match the specified criteria.
- **Shortest Path:** By clicking on two nodes, the system highlights the sequence of intermediate concepts and connecting edges that form the shortest directed path between them. This feature helps users trace conceptual dependencies and relationships within the lattice structure. The resulting path is visually emphasized using distinct colors, and the path summary is displayed just below the lattice.

To illustrate these exploration features, we present the well-known *Live-in-Water* formal context and its corresponding concept lattice visualization.

Table 2 shows the well-known *Live-in-Water* formal context, commonly used in FCA to illustrate conceptual structures. In this context, the rows represent objects (such as *dog* or *bean*), and the columns represent attributes (such as *lives in water* or *can move*). A value of "x" indicates that the object possesses the corresponding attribute.

The concept lattice shown in Fig. 2 visualizes the hierarchical structure derived from the *live-in-water* formal context presented in Table 2. In this visualization, each node represents a formal concept labeled with its extent (objects) and intent (attributes). The color coding follows a filtering scheme based on user-defined search criteria. Specifically, orange nodes indicate concepts that match both the specified extent and intent, green nodes highlight concepts that match only the extent, and grey nodes indicate a match on intent alone. Blue nodes represent concepts that do not match either filter criterion. This color-coded view supports targeted exploration of concept lattices by visually distinguishing relevant concepts from the rest of the structure.

Table 2. A formal context describing *live-in-water* [24].

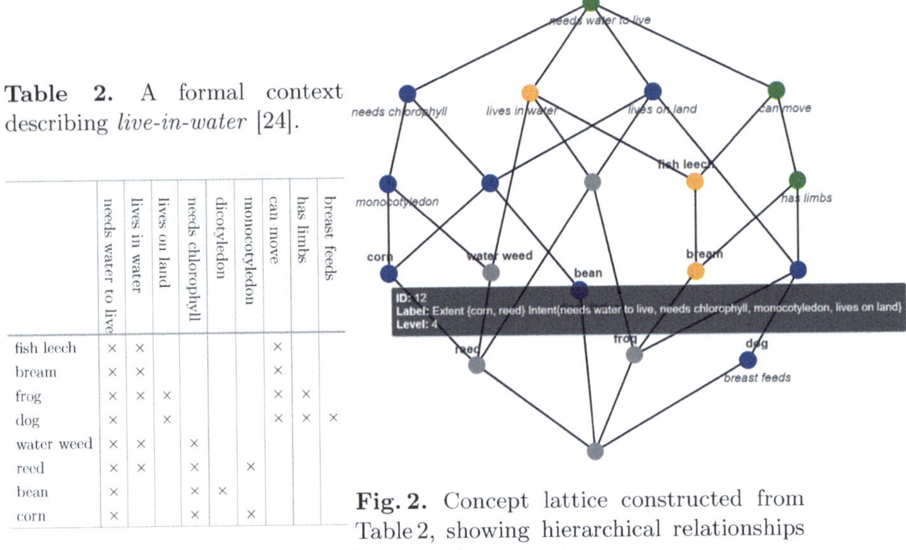

	needs water to live	lives in water	lives on land	needs chlorophyll	dicotyledon	monocotyledon	can move	has limbs	breast feeds
fish leech	×	×					×		
bream	×	×					×		
frog	×	×	×				×	×	
dog	×		×				×	×	×
water weed	×	×		×					
reed	×	×		×		×			
bean	×			×	×				
corn	×			×		×			

Fig. 2. Concept lattice constructed from Table 2, showing hierarchical relationships between the concepts.

4.3 Labeling Modes

`lattice.js` supports three labeling strategies to balance readability and information density depending on the user's needs:

- **Default Labeling:** By default, each concept is identified only by a unique ID. This minimal representation ensures clarity in dense lattices or during layout adjustments, but does not reveal any information about the concept's extent or intent.
- **Full Labeling:** Displays both the extent (objects) and intent (attributes) for each concept. While this provides a complete view of the concept's meaning, it

often leads to label redundancy, especially in large lattices, as shared elements are repeated across multiple concepts.
- **Reduced Labeling:** Reduced labeling improves readability by showing only the newly introduced objects and attributes at their most specific concept. This reduces redundancy and helps users interpret concepts more efficiently.

4.4 Structural Metric Computation

The library automatically computes both global and concept-level metrics, derived from the extent and intent information embedded in each concept's label, including:

- Total number of concepts, objects, and attributes.
- Lattice density, reflecting the ratio of actual to possible connections.
- The average stability across all concepts computed for the whole lattice
- Concept-level metrics such as extent size, intent size, stability (how strongly the concept is supported by its data), and neighborhood size (the number of direct connections).

These metrics are automatically computed during lattice generation and are made available both for interactive display and for further analysis.

4.5 File Handling and Export

`lattice.js` provides a comprehensive file handling system that supports importing, converting, and exporting concept lattice data. Users can upload JSON files through an intuitive interface, where the system parses the input, validates its structure, and generates the corresponding interactive visualization. This process automatically activates related features, including filtering, labeling, and metric computation.

To accommodate data from external FCA tools[3], the library includes a converter that transforms serialized FCA structures into a format suitable for direct visualization. The parser reconstructs nodes, assigns labels, restores superconcept–subconcept relationships, and determines layer assignments to maintain visual consistency. The converted data can also be exported as a normalized JSON file.

For documentation, sharing, or further analysis, *lattice.js* supports export in multiple formats: JSON, CSV, PNG and PDF.

4.6 Formal Context Viewer

Beyond visualizing concept lattices, `lattice.js` offers a formal context viewer that reconstructs the original binary context table from the current lattice data.

[3] https://concepts.readthedocs.io/en/stable/advanced.html#custom-serialization-format.

With a single click, users can generate a cross-table where rows represent objects and columns represent attributes. The system extracts each concept's extent and intent by parsing its label, then marks object–attribute pairs with a 1 wherever a relation exists. This reconstructed view allows users to verify the consistency between the visualized lattice and its underlying formal context, supporting both validation and educational purposes. In addition, users can export the reconstructed context directly in CSV and CXT formats, enabling integration with external FCA tools and workflows.

While `lattice.js` provides a rich set of features for visualizing and interacting with concept lattices, several challenges remain. The next section outlines current limitations of the tool and discusses planned improvements and future research directions.

5 Limitations and Future Work

Currently, `lattice.js` focuses exclusively on the visualization and interactive exploration of precomputed concept lattices. It does not yet include built-in functionalities for constructing concept lattices directly from formal contexts or for computing implication bases, which limits its applicability to workflows where lattice computation is handled externally.

Further development will focus on extending the library to support integrated lattice construction from formal contexts, enabling end-to-end FCA analysis within the same environment. Additionally, we plan to investigate 3D layout techniques to improve the visualization of large or dense lattices, reducing visual clutter through depth-based separation. Finally, our objective is to explore the integration of `lattice.js` with FCA tools and LLMs to support knowledge discovery, attribute exploration, and semi-automated extraction of the implication bases.

6 Conclusions

This paper presented `lattice.js`, a JavaScript library for interactive concept lattice visualization in the browser. By combining hierarchical layout algorithms with user-friendly interactive features such as zooming, filtering, node dragging, customizable labeling, shortest path computation, and structural metrics, the library enables accessible, intuitive and scalable exploration of FCA structures.

In addition to describing the libraryF's interface and functionalities, we described the layout algorithms that underpin the visualizations. We also introduced recent extensions, including shortest path computation and export of reconstructed formal contexts in CSV and CXT formats.

Future work will aim to extend the library with built-in support for computing concept lattices directly from formal contexts, incorporating 3D visualization techniques, and integrating implication base computation, attribute exploration, and Large Language Models (LLMs) to support semi-automated reasoning and knowledge discovery.

References

1. Alam, M., Napoli, A., Lévy, N., Toussaint, Y.: Latviz – a new practical tool for performing interactive exploration over concept lattices. In: 13th International Conference on CLA 2016, vol. 1624, pp. 9–20 (2016)
2. Andrews, S., Hirsch, L.: A tool for creating and visualising formal concept trees. In: CEUR Workshop Proceedings, vol. 1637, pp. 1–9 (2016)
3. Becker, P., Hereth, J., Stumme, G.: Toscanaj – an open source tool for qualitative data analysis. In: Workshop FCAKDD of the 15th ECAI 2002. Lyon, France (2002)
4. Belohlávek, R., Kwuida, L.: Lattice miner: a tool for concept lattice construction and exploration. In: ICFCA 2010. Canada (2010)
5. Borchmann, D.: Exploratory programming for FCA — an introduction to conexp-clj. In: Workshop for FCA Tools and Applications (FCA-Tools) (2013)
6. Borza, P.V., Sere, O., Stoean, C.: OpenFCA – an open source formal concept analysis toolbox. In: IC-AQTR 2010. Romania (2010)
7. Bostock, M., Ogievetsky, V., Heer, J.: D3 data-driven documents. IEEE Trans. Visual Comput. Graphics **17**(12), 2301–2309 (2011)
8. Chimani, M., Gutwenger, C., Jünger, M., Klau, G.W., Mutzel, P., Weiskircher, R.: The open graph drawing framework (OGDF). In: Handbook of Graph Drawing and Visualization, pp. 543–569. CRC Press (2013)
9. Coffman, E.G., Graham, R.L.: Optimal scheduling for two-processor systems. Acta Informatica **1**, 200–213 (1972)
10. Dürrschnabel, D., Hanika, T., Stumme, G.: Dimdraw – a novel tool for drawing concept lattices. In: ICFCA 2019. Frankfurt, Germany (2019)
11. Eades, P., Wormald, N.C.: Edge crossings in drawings of bipartite graphs. Algorithmica **11**, 379–403 (1994). https://doi.org/10.1007/BF01187020
12. Freese, R.: Automated lattice drawing. In: Eklund, P. (ed.) ICFCA 2004. LNCS (LNAI), vol. 2961, pp. 112–127. Springer, Heidelberg (2004). https://doi.org/10.1007/978-3-540-24651-0_12
13. Ganter, B., Wille, R.: Formal Concept Analysis: Mathematical Foundations. Springer, Heidelberg (1999). https://doi.org/10.1007/978-3-642-59830-2
14. Garey, M.R., Johnson, D.S.: Crossing number is NP-complete. SIAM J. Algebraic Discrete Methods **4**(3), 312–316 (1983)
15. Gutierrez, A., Huchard, M., Martin, P.: FCA4J: a java library for relational concept analysis and formal concept analysis. In: ETAFCA 2022, pp. 207–212 (2022)
16. Hanika, T., Hirth, J.: Conexp-clj – a research tool for FCA. In: Proceedings of the 15th International Conference on Formal Concept Analysis (ICFCA 2019) (2019)
17. Healy, P., Nikolov, N.S.: Hierarchical drawing algorithms. In: Tamassia, R. (ed.) Handbook of Graph Drawing and Visualization, pp. 409–446. CRC Press (2013)
18. Hodo, F., Balderas-Díaz, S., Guerrero-Contreras, G., Sertkaya, B.: lattice.js: A javascript library for interactive concept lattice visualization (2025). submitted for publication in: JIPII 2025, Cádiz
19. Mehdi, R., Emamirad, K.: Lattice miner – a formal concept analysis tool. In: ICFCA 2017. Rennes, France (2017)
20. Muller, E., Huchard, M., Martin, P., Poncelet, P., Sallaberry, A.: RCAviz: Visualizing and exploring relational conceptual structures. In: CLA 2022, pp. 135–148 (2022)
21. Priss, U.: Fcastone – FCA file format conversion and interoperability. In: Conceptual Structures Tool Interoperability Workshop (CS-TIW) (2008)

22. Sugiyama, K., Tagawa, S., Toda, M.: Methods for visual understanding of hierarchical system structures. IEEE Trans. Syst. Man Cybern. **11**(2), 109–125 (1981)
23. Valtchev, P., Grosser, D., Roume, C., Rouane Hacene, M.: Galicia: an open platform for lattices. In: ICCS Workshop on FCA Applications (2003)
24. Wille, R.: Liniendiagramme hierarchischer Begriffssysteme. Indeks Verlag, Studien zur Klassifikation (1984)
25. Wille, R.: Concept lattices and conceptual knowledge systems. Comput. Math. Appl. **23**(6–9), 493–515 (1992)
26. Yevtushenko, S.A.: System of data analysis "concept explorer" (in russian). In: 7th National Conference on Artificial Intelligence, pp. 127–134. Russia (2000)

AI Applications

Analysis of DeepFake Detection Through Semi-supervised Facial Attribute Labeling

Vittorio Stile[1(✉)], Roberto Caldelli[1,2], Gabriel Guerrero-Contreras[3], Sara Balderas-Díaz[3], and Inmaculada Medina-Bulo[3]

[1] Universitas Mercatorum, Rome, Italy
vittoriostile@gmail.com
[2] Interuniversity Consortium for Telecommunications - CNIT, Florence, Italy
[3] Department of Computer Science and Engineering, University of Cadiz, Cádiz, Spain

Abstract. This study investigates the correlation between misclassifications in DeepFake detection and high-level facial attributes. A pre-trained frame-level classifier is used to distinguish between manipulated and authentic video contents and its wrong predictions are analyzed in detail. To enrich the dataset, we automatically annotate each video with additional labels, including gender, hair color, hair length, ear visibility and ethnicity, using a semi-supervised facial attribute recognition pipeline. An analysis of how misclassified video segments cross-reference with the visual attribute labels to identify emerging patterns is provided. Valuable insights for future bias-aware training strategies and more interpretable DeepFake detection systems are finally given.

Keywords: DeepFake Detection · Facial Attribute Analysis · Misclassification Analysis · Semi-Supervised Labeling · FaceForensics++

1 Introduction

DeepFake technologies have rapidly evolved in recent years, posing increasing threats to digital security, privacy, and public trust. These synthetic media techniques are capable of generating highly realistic face-swapped or manipulated videos, making them difficult to distinguish from authentic content [12,13]. Despite substantial progress in DeepFake detection, current systems often struggle to generalize across different manipulation types and compression levels, especially in uncontrolled real-world conditions [9,10]. Traditional detection approaches, such as those based on frequency artifacts [4] or inconsistencies in facial dynamics, typically rely on fixed patterns that may not transfer well across datasets or manipulation methods, limiting their robustness [8,14]. Recent research has explored the use of interpretable features and semantic attributes to enhance model explainability and resilience [6,15]. However, these studies often depend on manual annotation or are limited in scope. Automatic facial

J. Schäfer and J. Boubeta-Puig (Eds.): SGSOACS 2025, CCIS 2831, pp. 73–88, 2026.
https://doi.org/10.1007/978-3-032-14816-2_6

attribute labeling techniques, particularly semi-supervised approaches, remain underexplored in the context of DeepFake detection. This motivates our work, in which we investigate whether there exists a correlation between prediction errors and high-level visual characteristics derived through semi-supervised attribute labeling. By identifying such patterns, our aim is to support the development of more bias-aware, interpretable, and generalizable DeepFake detection systems. This study aims to analyze if DeepFake detection algorithms depend on visual attributes and, consequently, if detection could be enhanced by the knowledge of these attributes estimated through an automatic attribute labeling. To address this, we apply a semi-supervised labeling approach to the *FaceForensics++* dataset [10] and integrate it into an image-level DeepFake detection pipeline. We aim to evaluate which visual facial attributes most influence classifier decisions on manipulated versus authentic content. Facial attribute information may be incorporated as auxiliary inputs or conditioning variables during training. For example, one could design a bias-aware classification pipeline, where a preliminary model estimates facial attributes and feeds this information into a secondary DeepFake classifier. Such strategies would allow the system to dynamically adjust its decision threshold based on the attribute-informed context. This paper introduces a DeepFake detection method that incorporates facial attributes. Section 1 covers the challenges of DeepFake detection and reviews related work. Section 2 details the methodology, including data preparation, model architecture, and training. Section 3 presents experimental results. Finally, Sect. 4 offers conclusions and future research directions.

1.1 Related Work

The effectiveness of Convolutional Neural Network (CNN)s in DeepFake detection was first demonstrated by *MesoNet* [1] and the *FaceForensics++* benchmark using *XceptionNet* [10]. Subsequent research has introduced enhancements such as spatio-temporal models [11], frequency-based features [4], and attention mechanisms [3]. Other studies incorporate multimodal signals like lip sync and compression artifacts [2]. Despite these advances, generalization remains a challenge. Several studies have recently explored interpretable and bias-aware approaches to DeepFake detection. For instance, [12] offers a comprehensive overview of face manipulation methods and detection techniques, including considerations of how certain manipulation strategies challenge generalization across datasets or focusing on interpretable semantic clues e.g., eye blinking [8]. More targeted efforts include [6], which introduces attention-based temporal features using recurrent neural networks, and [14], which proposes a method based on inconsistencies in head poses to detect forgeries. These works aim to improve detection accuracy through architectural or handcrafted cues directly embedded into the classifier. Similarly, [13] emphasizes the importance of robust forensics pipelines, highlighting limitations in detection systems under real-world variability. By contrast, our contribution is positioned differently. Rather than enhancing the detection model itself, we propose a systematic and empirical evaluation of its misclassification patterns through semi-supervised labeling of high-level visual attributes (e.g., gender, hair color, head visibility).

Our work extends this direction by applying structured facial attributes through semi-supervised labeling [15]. The labeling procedure is based on a self-learning method [7], who combine lightweight CNNs with inferred labels to adapt detection systems to evolving contexts. This work adopt semi-supervised facial attribute labeling as a foundation for a structured performance analysis of DeepFake detection models and validate it using both descriptive and statistical correlation metrics. While previous literature has explored the use of demographic or semantic features in detection or interpretability, no prior work has combined manual annotation and automated labeling in this fashion to investigate performance disparities. Our approach aims to uncover potential characteristics or appearance-related biases in post hoc prediction analysis, providing insights that can inform future fairness-aware model design. This novel strategy enables large-scale, interpretable evaluations and highlights potential biases in a replicable and extensible way.

2 The Proposed Methodology

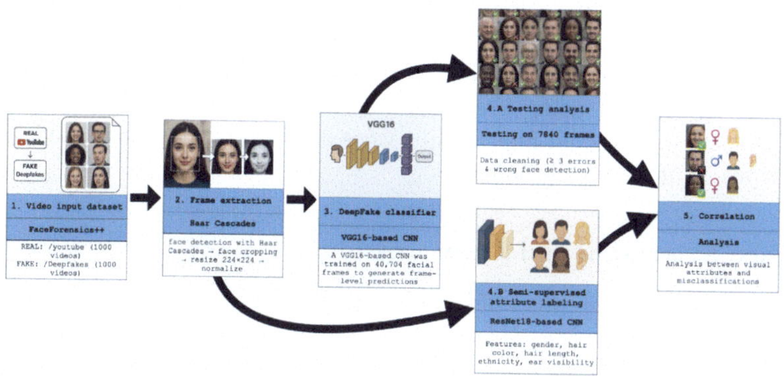

Fig. 1. Overview of the proposed methodology. The pipeline begins with video-level input from the FaceForensics++ dataset, proceeds through frame extraction and face cropping, followed by DeepFake classification at the frame level. A semi-supervised labeling process is then used to annotate facial attributes, and finally, correlations between those attributes and misclassification patterns are analyzed.

The methodology that has been followed primarily foresees to define a specific dataset containing real and DeepFake videos and then frames are extracted; these frames are successively processed and split into training, validation and test set in order to trained a neural network that is able to carry out an image-level classification task to distinguish between pristine and fake contents (see Fig. 1). In parallel, the test set which is used for the evaluation of the model has been labeled according to some facial attributes by resorting to a semi-supervised procedure. Based on the output of the labeling process, we investigate whether the predictions produced by the trained neural network exhibit systematic errors correlated with specific high-level facial attributes. Such possible relations could be exploited to improve DeepFake detection. Hereafter all the different phases of the adopted pipeline are described in detail.

2.1 Data Collection Phase

We utilized *FaceForensics++*, a benchmark dataset widely adopted in DeepFake research [10]. It consists of 1,000 pristine (REAL) videos collected from YouTube, stored in the `/youtube` directory, and named using a three-digit convention (e.g., `000.mp4`, `645.mp4`). These serve as source material for generating manipulated content across five different forgery types: *Deepfakes*, *NeuralTextures*, *FaceShifter*, *FaceSwap*, and *Face2Face*, each comprising 1,000 digitally altered versions of the original real videos and organized in separate folders. In this study, we selected the 1,000 REAL videos from the `/youtube` folder and their corresponding 1,000 FAKE videos from the `/Deepfakes` folder, focusing our analysis on this specific forgery method. All videos used in this study refer to the **C40 compression level**, a setting that applies moderate compression and has shown to produce stable and consistent detection performance across experiments. Accordingly, all reported results are based on this compression configuration. To enable frame-level classification, we converted the original video dataset into an image-based dataset. This was done by applying face detection techniques, specifically using Haar Cascades, on all videos in both REAL and FAKE categories. Detected face regions were cropped and resized, resulting in a large corpus of 56,000 facial images.

2.2 Face Extraction and Preprocessing

The objective of this preprocessing step was to extract face-only image frames from the FaceForensics++ dataset. Face detection was performed using the classical *Haar Cascades* method, the *OpenCV* `detectMultiScale` function was applied on grayscale versions of each frame. The `scaleFactor` parameter, set to 1.3, controls the image pyramid reduction ratio during face detection, enabling the model to detect faces at different scales. The `minNeighbors` parameter, set to 5, defines the minimum number of adjacent rectangles required to retain a detection, acting as a threshold for eliminating false positives. These values were selected empirically, balancing detection accuracy and noise reduction. Detected faces were cropped, resized to 224×224 pixels (standard size for CNNs) and saved as individual `.jpeg` files. While effective, this pipeline presents notable challenges in terms of data volume introducing complexity in terms of both storage and computational overhead during training. To mitigate this, we adopted a frame skipping strategy with a fixed sampling rate of `skip = 20`, meaning one frame was retained for every twenty. This choice was guided by two considerations: it preserves a sufficient level of temporal representation of the source videos and it reduces redundancy, helping to prevent overfitting and model bias from near-duplicate frames. The resulting dataset consists of 28,000 real facial frames extracted from the 1,000 videos in the *Youtube* folder and 28,000 fake facial frames extracted from the 1,000 *Deepfakes* videos. From this collection, we constructed three subsets for training, validation, and testing. The **training set** contains a total of 40,320 facial images, equally divided between FAKE (20,160) and REAL (20,160) instances. The **validation set** consists of 7,840 images, again balanced between classes. Similarly, the **test set** includes 7,840 images with an equal number of REAL and FAKE faces.

Although various convolutional neural networks were evaluated during the frame-level DeepFake detection phase, including architectures such as *ResNet50*, we ultimately report results only for the *VGG16*-based model. This decision stems from the observation that performance across different architectures was highly comparable in terms of accuracy, precision, and F1-score. The VGG16 model, initialized with ImageNet pre-trained weights and with all layers frozen during training, demonstrated reliable and consistent behavior, particularly on C40-compressed facial images and due to its ease of deployment on standard hardware[1], it was selected as the reference architecture for this study.

2.3 Labeling Phase

To annotate the dataset, a semi-supervised labeling approach was adopted [7]. As a first step, we established a ground truth by manually inspecting the first 50 REAL videos from the `/youtube` folder of the FaceForensics++ dataset, specifically those named from `000.mp4` to `049.mp4`. Each video was carefully reviewed, frame by frame, to assign a comprehensive set of high-level visual and semantic labels. The annotation included a range of categorical features such as `gender` (with values FEMALE or MALE), `ethnicity` (AFRICAN, ASIAN, MIXED, WHITE, OTHER), `expression` (ANGRY, DISGUSTED, HAPPY, LAUGHING, SERIOUS, SURPRISED), `hair_color` (BLONDE, BLACK, BROWN, GREY, LIGHT BROWN, RED, OTHER), `hair_length` (BALD, LONG, PONYTAIL, SHORT), `action` (HUGGING, STILL, WALKING) and `position` (SITTING, STANDING, UNKNOWN). In parallel, a set of boolean attributes was also collected, including indicators such as whether the subject is alone, whether the ears or forehead are visible, whether glasses are worn, and whether the video exhibits camera movement, pan effects, shakiness, or active talking, each having a TRUE or FALSE value. All labels were assigned based on visible and consistent traits throughout the selected video clips. For the purposes of this study, we assume that each manipulated video, generated from a corresponding real video via the DeepFakes method and located in the `/Deepfakes` folder, inherits the same attribute labels as its original. For example, if the REAL video `005.mp4` is labeled as having gender: FEMALE and hair_length: LONG, its

[1] For a standard hardware we refer to a consumer-grade computer: a MacBook Air equipped with an Apple M2 processor, 8-core CPU, 8-core GPU, 8GB of RAM.

corresponding DeepFake version `005_010.mp4` is assumed to retain these same properties.

These enriched labels were added to the original binary classification label `is_real`, which was the only ground truth available in the original FaceForensics++ dataset. The resulting annotated set aims to be a foundation for the development of more interpretable detection models. This initial annotated subset of 50 REAL videos serves as the foundation for training the attribute labeling models in the subsequent semi-supervised pipeline. Then using 5% (50 videos) of manually labeled instances from the youtube dataset, the self-labeling approach enables the generation of pseudolabels for the remaining 95% (950 videos). The auto-labeling process is based on a *ResNet18* backbone, trained separately for each visual attribute (visibility of ears, ethnicity, forehead coverage, gender, hair color and hair length) using a dedicated binary or multiclass classifier depending on the label type.

The training follows an iterative semi-supervised loop designed to progressively expand the labeled dataset. Initially, the manually annotated subset (50 videos) is partitioned into training, validation, and test splits following a 60-20-20 scheme (30-10-10 videos). In the first iteration, the pretrained *ResNet18* model is fine-tuned on the training set, using the validation set to prevent overfitting through an early stopping strategy. This fine-tuned model is then evaluated on the test split to establish the baseline performance. Additionally, it is employed to pseudolabel the remaining unlabeled data (950 videos), thereby generating an augmented training dataset comprising the 30 manually labeled videos and up to 950 pseudolabeled instances. Only pseudolabeled instances with a confidence score above 95% are added to the augmented dataset, which is then used to further fine-tune the pretrained *ResNet18*. This process of augmentation and retraining repeats until convergence on the test split or no additional high-confidence samples remain.

From an initial set of visual attributes, features such as gender, hair color, and ear visibility demonstrated high predictive power and were retained. Attributes with only one class (e.g., `is_real = True`, `is_glasses = False`) were excluded from training to prevent class imbalance. Table 1 provides an overview of the attributes selected to analyze the influence of specific visual features on DeepFake detection performance.

Table 1. Selected facial attributes used for analysis.

Attribute	Labels
`hair_color`	BLONDE, BLACK, BROWN, GREY, LIGHT BROWN, RED, OTHER
`hair_length`	BALD, LONG, PONYTAIL, SHORT
`gender`	FEMALE, MALE
`ethnicity`	AFRICAN, ASIAN, MIXED, WHITE, OTHER
`is_ears_visible`	TRUE, FALSE

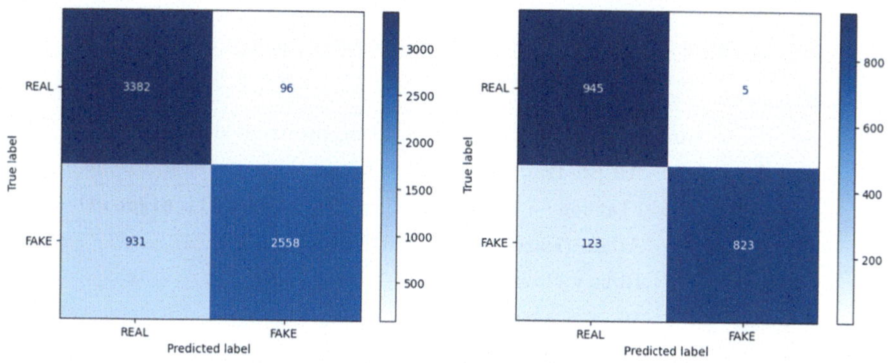

Fig. 2. Frame-based Confusion Matrix.

Fig. 3. Video-based Confusion Matrix.

2.4 Detection Phase

The experimental evaluation aimed to assess the effectiveness of our DeepFake detection pipeline based on visual features extracted from facial frames. The model was trained on a balanced dataset of 40,320 facial images (20,160 REAL and 20,160 FAKE), with a validation set of 7,840 images (equally split between classes), and a test set of 7,840 frames also balanced across the two classes, as shown in Table 2.

The classifier was based on the VGG16 architecture, with pre-trained ImageNet weights and all convolutional layers frozen. A simple custom head was added, consisting of a `Flatten` layer followed by `Dense(512, relu)` and a final `Dense(1, sigmoid)` output. Training was performed with the Adam optimizer (learning rate = 0.0001), binary cross-entropy loss, batch size of 16, and 5 epochs. The complete configuration is reported in Table 3. After training, the model reached a training accuracy of 94.58% and a validation accuracy of 86.96%. The test set was then used to evaluate the final model. Prior to evaluation, a face filtering step was applied to include only the primary detected face per video, referred to as `face0`. This is based on the assumption that in most cases, `face0`

Table 2. Dataset split by set and class.

Set	REAL	FAKE	Total
Training	20,160	20,160	40,320
Validation	3,920	3,920	7,840
Test	3,920	3,920	7,840

Table 3. Model architecture and training configuration.

Component	Details
Base architecture	VGG16 (`include_top=False`, pre-trained on *ImageNet*)
Frozen layers	All pre-trained layers are frozen
Custom head	`Flatten` → `Dense(512, relu)` → `Dense(1, sigmoid)`
Optimizer	Adam (learning rate = 0.0001)
Loss function	Binary Crossentropy
Batch size	16
Epochs	5

corresponds to the main subject, which is typically the manipulation target.[2] The resulting filtered test set consisted of 6,967 frames, corresponding to 950 REAL videos and 946 FAKE videos.

The model's frame-level classification performance is summarized in Table 4, and the confusion matrix is illustrated in Fig. 2. These results highlight the model's precision in detecting FAKE content (96.38%) and its strong recall for REAL frames (97.24%), with overall balanced performance across both classes. The performance of the model on the frame-level test set (`face0`-only) resulted in an accuracy of 85.26% across 6,967 frames. This confirms the model's strong generalization capability, particularly its high recall on REAL frames and precision on FAKE ones, as detailed in Table 4 and visualized in the confusion matrix in Fig. 2. Although classification is performed at the frame level, system reliability in DeepFake detection is typically evaluated at the video level. According to established literature, it is not methodologically sound to mark an entire video as misclassified based on a single erroneous frame. Rössler et al. [10] and Sabir et al. [11] suggest aggregation strategies such as mean score, majority voting, or top-K frame voting to derive a more robust video-level decision.

Table 4. Frame-level classification report on the face0-only test set.

Class	Precision	Recall	F1-score	Support
REAL	0.7841	0.9724	0.8682	3478
FAKE	0.9638	0.7332	0.8328	3489
Total frames				6967

[2] In videos where multiple faces are detected, Haar Cascades assigns incremental indices such as `face0`, `face1`, `face2`, etc. The first detected face (`face0`) is usually the one that appears most prominently and is therefore selected as the representative frame.

A widely accepted criterion in the literature considers a video to be misclassified only if it contains *at least three wrongly predicted frames*, or if a *significant proportion* of its frames (typically $\geq$10%) are incorrect. This threshold is particularly appropriate in our case, as each video in the test set contains an average of 28 extracted frames. Adopting this strategy helps mitigate the impact of isolated frame-level anomalies and enables a more robust and representative evaluation. As a direct consequence, we avoid marking as erroneous a large portion of the dataset composed of 284 videos with only one misclassified frame and 115 videos with exactly two misclassified frames. These videos will henceforth be considered correctly classified in all subsequent video-based analyses. In addition to this literature-based thresholding, we further examined the distribution of wrongly predicted frames per video. Some videos exhibited disproportionately high error counts, as illustrated in Fig. 8. To better understand these outliers, we isolated the subset of 13 videos with more than five misclassified frames and manually analyzed each one through visual inspection. Among these, several were found to exhibit specific singularities. In video `548_632`, the frame labeled as `face0` corresponds to a background face depicted within a picture frame as can be seen in the Fig. 7. Although the video is labeled as FAKE, this face is not the actual DeepFake target; the model correctly classifies it as REAL, thus introducing misleading noise. Similarly, in video `305_513` as can be seen in the Fig. 5, two faces are present, and the one identified as `face0` is not the manipulated subject. Lastly, in video `554_572` as can be seen in the Fig. 6, the main detected face corresponds to a shadow (like reflection on the wall) again, not the DeepFake target.

To ensure dataset integrity, we excluded these three videos from the subsequent analysis. We also discarded all videos with fewer than three wrongly predicted frames, following the threshold rationale described earlier. The video `186_170.mp4` shows a television anchorwoman with additional faces on a background screen (Fig. 4), but in this case the target face of the DeepFake has been correctly identified and therefore this does not lead to spurious detections unrelated to the manipulated subject.

Fig. 4. Video `186_170.mp4`, many faces but the main face is recognized correctly.

Fig. 5. Video `305_513.mp4`, the main face is not the target of the DeepFake.

Fig. 6. Video `554_572.mp4`, a face in a photograph in the background is recognized as main face.

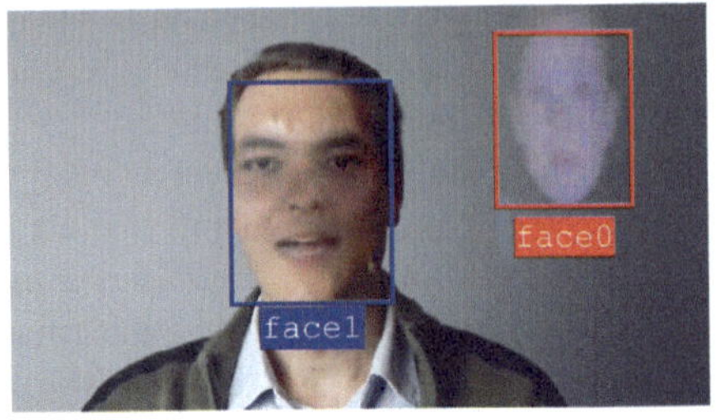

Fig. 7. Video `548_632.mp4`, a shadow face in the background is recognized as the main face.

Table 5. Video-based classification report.

Class	Precision	Recall	F1-score	Videos
REAL	0.8848	0.9947	0.9366	950
FAKE	0.9605	0.6807	0.9278	946
Total				1896

To better reflect real-world deployment conditions, where decisions are typically made at the video level rather than per frame, we aggregated predictions by assigning each video the label associated with its corresponding `face0` frame. This aggregation yielded a test set consisting of 950 REAL videos and 946 FAKE videos. Among these, after defining criteria for classifying a video as mispredicted and analyzing several edge cases, a total of 128 videos were identified as misclassified at the video level. These misclassified instances are characterized by containing between 3 and 8 wrongly predicted frames, indicating a consistent frame-level ambiguity within those videos. The distribution of videos based on the number of frame-level mispredictions is illustrated in Fig. 9. When tested at this video granularity, the system achieved a video-based test accuracy of 93.25% over 1,896 videos. This substantial improvement over the frame-level result confirms the robustness of `face0` as a representative frame for classification. The resulting confusion matrix is shown in Fig. 3, while a detailed classification report for video-based predictions is presented in Table 5. This analysis offers a more application-driven perspective on the effectiveness of the system in practice, where predictions are typically needed per video unit.

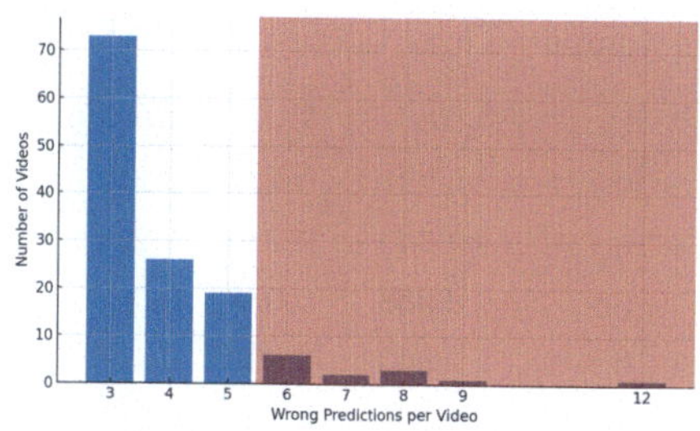

Fig. 8. Distribution of Videos by Number of Wrong Predictions Including Misleading Videos.

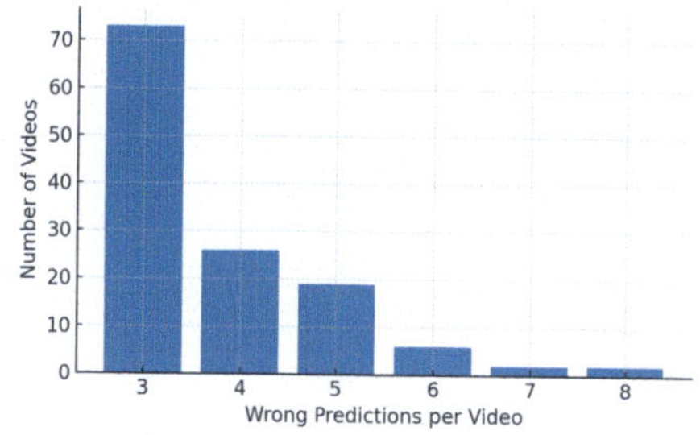

Fig. 9. Distribution of Videos by Number of Wrong Predictions Excluding Misleading Videos.

3 Analysis of the Relations Between Labels and Wrong Predictions

To investigate the presence of biases linked to specific visual attributes, we conducted a quantitative analysis correlating classification errors with demographic and appearance-based labels. We computed standard performance metrics, precision, recall, F1-score, and error rate, for each category within five key features: gender, ethnicity, hair color, hair length, and ear visibility. These metrics provide complementary insights: *precision* (Prec) indicates the proportion of correct predictions among all predictions for a label, *recall* (Rec) measures the ability to correctly detect all instances of that label, and *F1-score* (F1) balances both. The *error rate* (ER) reflects the proportion of misclassified instances out of the total for each label. The complete results are shown in Table 6.

A few patterns clearly emerge. First, individuals labeled with `LONG` hair show the highest F1-score (0.76), compared to `SHORT` hair (0.69), suggesting that the model performs more reliably on longer hairstyles. Conversely, videos featuring subjects with `SHORT` hair present the highest error rate (30%), indicating a potential challenge for the model in processing these cases. Gender-wise, the model shows slightly better performance on `FEMALE` (F1-score: 0.74) compared to `MALE` (F1-score: 0.72), although the difference is marginal. Notably, the most frequent ethnicity in the dataset, `WHITE`, also has a relatively high error rate (26.9%), which may reflect overfitting to this majority class or hidden variance in the visual features within that group. On the other hand, labels with very few samples (e.g., `BALD`, `OTHER` for hair color, or `PONYTAIL`) display perfect or near-perfect scores. However, this should not be interpreted as strong model performance, as their sample sizes are too small to draw statistically reliable conclusions. Overall, the analysis reveals some signs of performance disparity across features. While no overwhelming bias is detected, attributes such as `SHORT` hair and `WHITE` ethnicity warrant closer scrutiny in further analysis to assess whether augmenting underperforming subgroups could improve fairness in DeepFake detection.

To deepen explore potential biases in the DeepFake detection pipeline, we computed three statistical correlation metrics between the presence of misclas-

Table 6. Label-wise classification metrics computed over the test video set.

Feature	Label	Videos n°	Prec (↑)	Rec (↑)	F1 (↑)	ER (↓)
gender	MALE	774	0.721	0.721	0.721	0.279
gender	FEMALE	1226	0.746	0.746	0.746	0.254
ethnicity	OTHER	16	0.938	0.938	0.938	0.063
ethnicity	ASIAN	66	0.803	0.803	0.803	0.197
ethnicity	WHITE	1890	0.731	0.731	0.731	0.269
ethnicity	AFRICAN	14	0.786	0.786	0.786	0.214
ethnicity	MIXED	14	0.857	0.857	0.857	0.143
hair_color	OTHER	4	0.750	0.750	0.750	0.250
hair_color	BLACK	1482	0.735	0.735	0.735	0.265
hair_color	GREY	112	0.741	0.741	0.741	0.259
hair_color	BROWN	102	0.686	0.686	0.686	0.314
hair_color	LIGHT BROWN	26	0.731	0.731	0.731	0.269
hair_color	BLONDE	286	0.727	0.727	0.727	0.273
hair_length	LONG	1056	0.763	0.763	0.763	0.237
hair_length	SHORT	936	0.700	0.700	0.700	0.300
hair_length	BALD	4	0.750	0.750	0.750	0.250
hair_length	PONYTAIL	4	1.000	1.000	1.000	0.000
is_ears_visible	TRUE	1618	0.737	0.737	0.737	0.263
is_ears_visible	FALSE	382	0.723	0.723	0.723	0.277

sifications (wrong predictions) and each attribute label: *Chi-square test statistic* (Eq. 1), *p-value*, and *Mutual Information (MI)* (Eq. 2). Given Observed Frequence (O) and Expected Frequence (E) from which consequently O_{ij} and E_{ij} for cell (i, j), the *Chi-square* statistic is defined as

$$\chi^2 = \sum_i \sum_j \frac{(O_{ij} - E_{ij})^2}{E_{ij}} \tag{1}$$

and the resulting p-value estimates the probability that a discrepancy at least as large could arise under the null hypothesis of independence. The conventional decision rule adopts the threshold $p < 0.05$ to claim statistical significance [5]. Complementarily, MI quantifies how much information the attribute label X conveys about the correctness indicator Y:

$$MI(X,Y) = \sum_x \sum_y p(x,y) \log\left(\frac{p(x,y)}{p(x)\,p(y)}\right) \tag{2}$$

The *Chi-square* test measures the discrepancy between the observed and expected distributions of categorical variables, indicating whether the error rate is uniformly distributed across attribute labels. The *p-value* represents the probability that any observed difference is due to chance. A threshold of $p < 0.05$ is commonly adopted to denote statistical significance [5]. Lastly, *MI* quantifies how much knowing one variable (e.g., the label) reduces the uncertainty about the other (e.g., prediction correctness). Higher MI values imply stronger dependence. The results are summarized in Table 7. Notably, the attribute `hair_length` stands out with a statistically significant p-value of 0.031793, suggesting that the likelihood of a wrong prediction is not evenly distributed across different hair length categories. This supports earlier classification metrics where `SHORT` hair length was associated with the highest error rate (30.04%).

Table 7. Statistical correlation metrics between features and wrong predictions.

Feature	Chi-Square	p-value	MI
gender	1.449053	0.228680	0.000393
ethnicity	6.332719	0.175640	0.001902
hair_color	3.999698	0.779812	0.001166
hair_length	10.573959	0.031793	0.003107
is_ears_visible	1.190591	0.275210	0.000328

Expanding upon the previous analysis, which examined overall model performance using Precision, Recall, F1-Score and Error Rate as well as statistical correlation metrics by attribute category, we now explore these relationships at a finer granularity. Specifically, we assess bias in model misclassifications by analyzing individual label values for each attribute.

The results, summarized in Table 8, indicate that the label `hair_length = SHORT` exhibits a statistically significant correlation with misclassifications ($p < 0.05$), suggesting a potential association between this attribute and increased prediction errors. While `ethnicity = WHITE` also shows statistical significance, this finding should be interpreted with caution. Given that this label is overwhelmingly dominant in the dataset, the higher error count may primarily reflect its prevalence rather than a specific model weakness toward this subgroup. Notably, `hair_length = LONG`, although above the threshold for statistical significance, stands out due to its performance in prior metrics, showing the highest F1-score (0.76) among hair length categories. This supports the idea that this label may be a particularly meaningful feature for DeepFake detection and warrants further investigation as a potentially informative trait rather than a source of model bias. These results emphasize the importance of considering label distribution when evaluating bias and suggest that more balanced datasets or stratified analyses are needed to isolate the true effect of features on prediction performance.

Table 8. Label-wise statistical correlation metrics with wrong predictions.

Feature	Label	Chi-Square	p-value	MI
gender	MALE	1.4491	0.2287	0.0000
gender	FEMALE	1.4491	0.2287	0.0143
ethnicity	OTHER	2.3948	0.1217	0.0000
ethnicity	ASIAN	1.2224	0.2689	0.0059
ethnicity	WHITE	4.4596	0.0347	0.0000
ethnicity	AFRICAN	0.0132	0.9084	0.0000
ethnicity	MIXED	0.5240	0.4691	0.0000
hair_color	OTHER	0.0000	1.0000	0.0000
hair_color	BLACK	0.0533	0.8174	0.0000
hair_color	GREY	0.0000	0.9979	0.0000
hair_color	BROWN	1.1377	0.2861	0.0000
hair_color	LIGHT BROWN	0.6108	0.4345	0.0000
hair_color	BLONDE	0.1414	0.7069	0.0139
hair_color	RED	0.0019	0.9654	0.0000
hair_length	LONG	3.5820	0.0584	0.0098
hair_length	SHORT	6.0163	0.0142	0.0000
hair_length	BALD	0.0000	1.0000	0.0000
hair_length	PONYTAIL	2.3158	0.1281	0.0043
is_ears_visible	FALSE	1.1906	0.2752	0.0148
is_ears_visible	TRUE	1.1906	0.2752	0.0000

4 Conclusions and Future Works

This preliminary study validates the feasibility of enriching DeepFake detection pipelines with automatically labeled facial attributes obtained via a semi-supervised learning process. This work contributes to the DeepFake detection community in three ways: (1) it presents a semi-supervised attribute labeling strategy applicable at scale, (2) it identifies performance disparities across attribute subgroups, and (3) it highlights critical areas where bias mitigation should be prioritized in future detection pipelines. Our results demonstrate that such auxiliary information based on visual attributes can support improved detection.

Future works will be dedicated to better understand how such side information could be adopted during the model training phase to support DeepFake detection and, based on the result detailed in Sect. 3 should therefore enlarge the representation of short-haired subjects, enrich ear-occlusion scenarios, and incorporate fairness-aware regularisers to guarantee balanced performance across hairstyle and visibility conditions. While our current analysis employs classical significance testing (*chi-square* and MI), in future extensions we plan to apply multivariate analyses, such as logistic regression with interaction terms, generalized linear models or causal inference frameworks, on balanced datasets to better understand interaction effects between features and improve generalizability of the findings to model the interdependencies among attributes and error outcomes more precisely. To promote transparency and encourage further research, we make available all resources required to replicate our experiments[3].

Acknowledgments. This work was partially supported by the project 21-FIN/RIC (Fin. Comp. 2024 UM). The authors would like to thank *PwC Business Services Srl* for supporting this activity. This publication is also part of the I+D+i grant PID2021-122215NB- C33 funded by MICIU/AEI/10.13039/501100011033 and by ERDF/EU.

References

1. Afchar, D., Nozick, V., Yamagishi, J., Echizen, I.: Mesonet: a compact facial video forgery detection network. In: 2018 IEEE International Workshop on Information Forensics and Security (WIFS), pp. 1–7. IEEE (2018)
2. Chandrasegaran, S.R., Xu, M., Mandal, B.: Cross-modal deepfake detection using inconsistent audio-visual cues. In: Proceedings of the IEEE/CVF Conference on Computer Vision and Pattern Recognition Workshops, pp. 1–9 (2021)
3. Dang, H., Liu, F., Stehouwer, H., Liu, X., Jain, A.K.: Detection of deepfake videos using multi-attentional convolutional neural networks. In: European Conference on Computer Vision, pp. 660–676. Springer (2020)
4. Durall, R., Keuper, M., Keuper, J.: Watch your step: learning a frequency-aware deepfake detector. arXiv preprint arXiv:2005.12496 (2020)
5. Fisher, R.A.: Statistical Methods for Research Workers. Oliver and Boyd, Edinburgh (1925)
6. Guera, D., Delp, E.J.: Deepfake video detection using recurrent neural networks. In: 2018 15th IEEE International Conference on Advanced Video and Signal Based Surveillance (AVSS), pp. 1–6. IEEE, Auckland, New Zealand (2018). https://doi.org/10.1109/AVSS.2018.8639163. https://ieeexplore.ieee.org/document/8639163/
7. Guerrero-Contreras, G., Balderas-Díaz, S., García-Pascual, A., Muñoz, A.: Adaptive vehicle detection in urban environments: a self-learning approach. In: Software Engineering and Formal Methods, pp. 39–52. Springer (2025)
8. Li, Y., Chang, M.C., Lyu, S.: In ictu oculi: exposing ai created fake videos by detecting eye blinking. In: 2018 IEEE International Workshop on Information Forensics and Security (WIFS), pp. 1–7. IEEE (2018)
9. Li, Y., Chang, M.C., Lyu, S.: Celeb-df: a new dataset for deepfake forensics. In: IEEE Conference on Computer Vision and Pattern Recognition (CVPR), pp. 3207–3216 (2020)
10. Rössler, A., Cozzolino, D., Verdoliva, L., Riess, C., Thies, J., Nießner, M.: Faceforensics++: learning to detect manipulated facial images. In: Proceedings of the IEEE/CVF International Conference on Computer Vision, pp. 1–11 (2019)

[3] URL to be added upon publication.

11. Sabir, E., Cheng, W., Jaiswal, A., AbdAlmageed, W., Masi, I., Natarajan, P.: Recurrent convolutional strategies for face manipulation detection in videos. In: Proceedings of the IEEE/CVF Conference on Computer Vision and Pattern Recognition Workshops, pp. 1–9 (2019)
12. Tolosana, R., Vera-Rodriguez, R., Fierrez, J., Morales, A., Ortega-Garcia, J.: Deepfakes and beyond: a survey of face manipulation and fake detection. Inf. Fusion **64**, 131–148 (2020)
13. Verdoliva, L.: Media forensics and deepfakes: an overview. IEEE J. Sel. Top. Signal Process. **14**(5), 910–932 (2020)
14. Yang, X., Li, Y., Lyu, S.: Exposing deep fakes using inconsistent head poses. In: ICASSP 2019-2019 IEEE International Conference on Acoustics, Speech and Signal Processing (ICASSP), pp. 8261–8265. IEEE (2019)
15. Zhang, N., Paluri, M., Ranzato, M., Darrell, T., Bourdev, L.: Panda: pose aligned networks for deep attribute modeling. In: Proceedings of the IEEE Conference on Computer Vision and Pattern Recognition, pp. 1637–1644 (2014)

Temporal Fusion Transformers for Forecasting ECG Signals

Fatima Sajid Butt(✉), Chitra Khatri, Aniket Prakash Nighot, and Matthias F. Wagner

Frankfurt University of Applied Sciences, Nibelungenplatz 1, 60318 Frankfurt am Main, Germany

fatima.butt@fra-uas.de, chitra.khatri@stud.fra-uas.de, aniket.nighot@stud.fra-uas.de, mfwagner@fra-uas.de

Abstract. Forecasting time series is a classical challenge in time series analysis. Applying machine learning based forecasting on the biomedical electrocardiogram (ECG) signals is not common but vital in predicting the overall health assessment of an individual. In this study, we forecast ECG signals using temporal fusion transformers (TFT) for the very first time. We use the renowned publicly available dataset, PTB-XL, to forecast all of the 12 leads. Different hyper parameters are used with temporal fusion transformer obtain optimal results. We downsample and normalize our dataset in order to reduce computational complexity as part of pre processing. Then it is fed into a TFT with different hyperparameter settings. We get an average root mean square error of 0.061 and mean absolute error of 0.128. The promising results encourage the application of TFTs for forecasting of ECG signals specifically for a better explainability emphasizing the research in explainable artificial intelligence (XAI).

Keywords: Temporal fusion networks · Electrocardiogram · Time Series Analysis · Forecasting

1 Introduction

Time Series Forecasting is prevalent in signal processing generally for fields like finance, human activity recognition but also specifically for medical domain where safety and precision is vital. It involves the estimation of future values of a signal derived from historic data.

Traditional time-series forecasting methodologies like ARIMA or exponential smoothing techniques etc. rely on the statistical and parametric approaches rooted in domain-specific knowledge. Machine learning and deep learning techniques, on the other hand, approach the forecasting mainly from a data centric alternative by autonomously learning temporal dependencies from large datasets.

Forecasting biomedical signals like ECG is important for several critical reasons. Predicting important medical events before they occur enables early interventions and potentially saves lives. Long term forecasting can help in monitoring

J. Schäfer and J. Boubeta-Puig (Eds.): SGSOACS 2025, CCIS 2831, pp. 89–98, 2026.
https://doi.org/10.1007/978-3-032-14816-2_7

abnormal heart activities like arrhythmia, myocardial infraction, tachycardia etc. before their occurrence. Similarly, short term real time prediction can assist in anticipating changes in ECG pattern in near future. Even though it is a vital use case to use ECG signals for forecasting signals, it is still less explored.

Temporal fusion transformers were introduced by Lim et al. [4] as an extension of transformers for multi-horizon forecasting. The model gives interpretable insights in to the temporal dynamics which are vital to understand the forecasting in medical domain. Classical models like ARIMA, SARIMA etc. are not suitable for forecasting complex and multivariate signals like ECGs. On the other hand, deep learning models like LSTMs suffer from higher computational demands, sensitivity to hyperparameter tuning, and potential for overfitting etc. while forecasting and also have no explainability capability. TFT is suitable for multivariate forecasting particularly for medical use-cases where, for example, when we need to predict different ECG channels either simultaneously or individually. TFT specializes in multi-horizon time series forecasting which essentially means it takes into account interdependency between different channels or dimensions as well for prediction.

The main motivation for this study is to prepare a model that uses TFTs for automatic ECG forecasting by learning the structure of the signal without heavy pre-processing. The proposed model can be used to predict effective insights for both long term and short term forecasting. In this study, we propose for the first time, to the best of our knowledge, using TFTs on ECG dataset.

2 Background and the State of the Art

For readers convenience, some of the technologies employed during this study are described briefly below:

Time series Forecasting has been a classical problem in time series modeling spanning multiple application areas like weather [1], financial market [3] and biomedical signals like ECG [2] and EEG signals.

A *time series* is a sequence of real-valued observations x indexed by time: $\{x_t\}_{t=1}^{T} = x_1, x_2, \ldots, x_T =\{x_1,\ x_2,\ \ldots,\ x_T\ \}$ where $x_t \in \mathbb{R}$ represents the value of the variable at time t, and T is the total number of time steps observed.

The goal of time series forecasting is to predict future values $\{x_{T+1}, x_{T+2}, \ldots,$ $x_{T+H}\}$ given the past observations:

$$\hat{x}_{T+h} = f(x_1, x_2, \ldots, x_T), \quad for \quad \{h = 1, 2, \ldots, H\}$$

where f is the forecasting function or model and H is the forecast horizon.

For multivariate time series, where each observation is a vector $\mathbf{x}_t \in \mathbb{R}^d$, we define:

$$\mathbf{x}_t = (x_t^{(1)}, x_t^{(2)}, \ldots, x_t^{(d)})$$

and the forecasting function becomes:

$$\hat{\mathbf{x}}_{T+h} = f(\mathbf{x}_1, \ldots, \mathbf{x}_T)$$

Many deep learning models have been designed with the aim of time series forecasting like LSTMs [10], Gated Recurrent Units and x-LSTMTime [5] based on [6].

TFT is designed upon a transformer architecture to efficiently build feature representation for different input types like static, known and observed inputs. The architecture consists of components like Gating mechanism, variable selection networks, static covariate encoders, temporal processing, and prediction intervals as shown in Fig. 1. We used TFT primarily because of its insights into explainability.

Zacarias et al. [11] applied traditional LSTMs for forecasting on Physionet ECG database, called MIT-BIH and achieved promising metric values of 0.0522 and 0.0070 as mean absolute error (MAE) and root mean square error (RMSE) respectively.

Kapral et al. [8] used a temporal fusion transformer (TFT) to forecast the blood pressure time series during surgery for up to 7 min in advance. The TFT was trained with low resolution data and showed excellent performance in predicting intraoperative hypotension in an adapted version.

Similarly [12] used TFT for the prediction of vital sign such as heart rate (HR), respiratory rate (RR), and peripheral oxygen saturation (SpO2) trajectories in intensive care patients.

Yang et al. [9] compared classical methods (ARIMA, VARIMA) with the performance of TFTs for the prediction of population-wide depression incidence. Their results provide a decision making framework for model selection and show superior performance of the TFT for various data structures.

In this paper, to the best of our knowledge, we use for the first time the forecasting model using TFTs for ECG prediction.

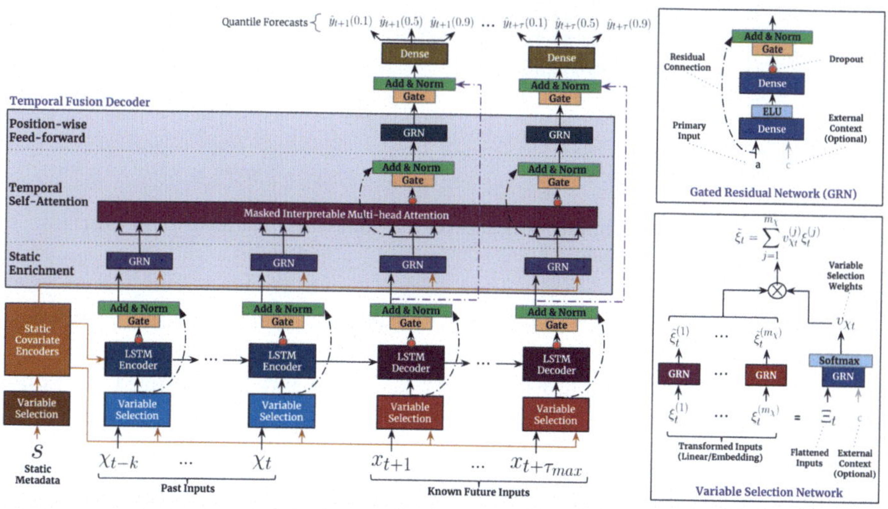

Fig. 1. The original layout of temporal fusion transformers as presented in [4].

3 Experimental Setup and Methodology

The PTB-XL dataset was published by Physikalisch-Technische Bundesanstalt (PTB) and is a large publicly available dataset. It contains 12-lead ECG recordings from more than 18000 patients annotated by cardiologists. PTB-XL includes both raw waveform data and rich metadata such as age, gender, and diagnosis classes (e.g., myocardial infarction, conduction disturbance, hypertrophy). Its scale, clinical diversity, and detailed labeling make it highly suitable for training and evaluating deep learning models for tasks such as arrhythmia detection, ECG classification, and forecasting [13]. PTB XL was used in our study because of its volume and the metadata available along with it. PyTorch was used along with libraries like wfdb, Pandas, Numpy, Pytorch_forecasting, torch, sklearn etc. The experiments were run on a high computational machine NVIDIA A100 GPU and on an Apple MacBook Pro M1MAX.

Data is processed to be create an individual row for each time index. As part of the data reduction, original ECG signals recorded at 1000 Hz are down sampled to 500 Hz by removing alternate rows for some experiment. This reduces computational complexity while preserving essential characteristics. Furthermore, ECG data is normalized using TorchNormalizer with robust scaling to handle outliers.

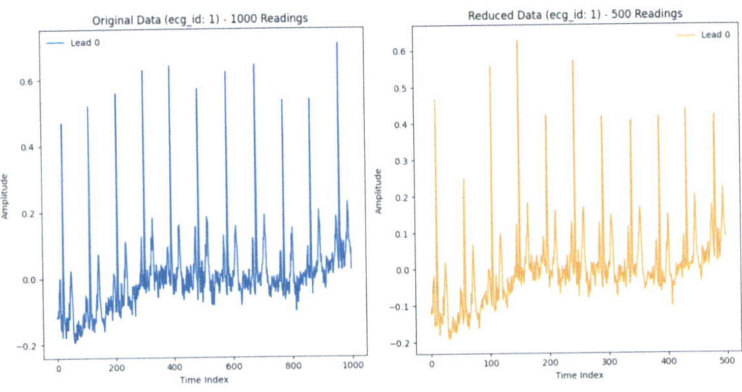

Fig. 2. Down sampled Signal: Original on left and down sampled data on right.

After the pre-processing, the dataset is split into training (80%), validation (10%), and test (10%) sets. Age and sex are chosen as Static features since they are constant for one patient. ECG leads and time index were used as Time-varying features.

4 TFT Fine Tuning

For the training and forecasting performance of a TFT the fine tuning of the hyper parameters is a crucial phase. The different components have to achieve optimal functioning without over- or underfitting and reaching computational efficiency. In the following section, some tradeoffs in the tuning of the most important hyper parameters are elaborated.

4.1 Impact of the LSTM Layer Number

The first layer of a multilayered LSTM stack in the TFT model might capture low-level patterns, while subsequent layers can combine these patterns to get more complex relationships. Using multiple LSTM layers allows the model to learn more complex non-linear associations in the time series. The hidden size parameter scales the capacity within each LSTM layer, but it does not increase the learning of hierarchical patterns. In a multilayered LSTM stack the lower levels focus on fine-grained details and the upper levels on broader trends.

4.2 Attention Head Size

The attention head size (related to the dimensions of the Key, Query, and Value matrices) controls the expressiveness of the attention mechanism. It determines how much information can be encoded and compared within the attention weights. Larger attention head sizes allow the model to capture more sophisticated relationships between different time steps and long-range dependencies. The TFT's attention mechanism is the primary mechanism for fusing information from multivariate time series and other variables.

4.3 Regularization

LSTM-based models are prone to overfitting. Therefore regularization methods like dropout and early stopping are important.

4.4 Batch Size

For training and forecasting larger batch sizes result in better parallelization and speed but higher memory requirements, which could be tremendous especially during training.

5 Results and Discussion

Several experiments were done to tune TFT in different ways. Table 1 presents an overview of all the experiments done. We chose mean absolute error (MAE) and root mean square error (RMSE) and Symmetric Mean Absolute Percentage Error (SMAPE) as metrics. It is seen that although MAE and RMSE are significantly lower but SMAPE is relatively higher. This indicates that either model requires more improvement or prediction window can be smaller for better prediction. In experiments 1–3 a prediction window of 150 time steps was used using 300 historic time steps. Experiment 1–4 were carried out on a NVIDIA A100 GPU and experiment 5 was performed on a MPS GPU on an Apple MacBook Pro M1MAX. Similarly learning rate was determined using learning rate finder (lr_find) from PyTorch Tuner library. One of the ECG signals along with the forecasting component is shown in Fig. 2. As it can be seen, the initial signals are forecasted very well and captures the trend of the signal appropriately. However as we move further in the prediction window, R peak predictions start to disappear. This indicates that in future experiments, we have to rearrange our prediction window. Since, the TFT has built in capability for XAI directly, we also looked initially into the variable importance generated by the model. The static variable importance generated by TFT provides an insight into relative importance of the variables. The largest contribution is to the $lead\_1$ scale. Also sex also plays a vital role in prediction (Figs. 3, 4, 5 and 6).

Table 1. Overview of different experiments with corresponding metrics

Experiment No.	MAE	RMSE	SMAPE
Experiment 1	0.0604	0.1234	0.9950
Experiment 2	0.0537	0.1184	0.9333
Experiment 3	0.0504	0.1135	0.8791
Experiment 4	0.0725	0.1466	1.0104
Experiment 5	0.0674	0.1402	0.962

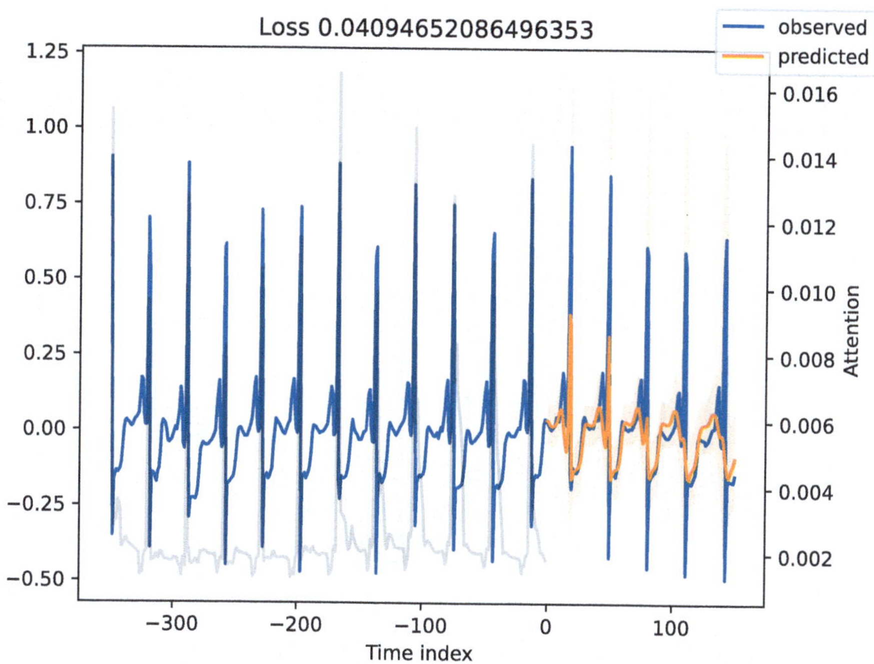

Fig. 3. Predicted (orange) vs. actual Lead 1 ECG (blue), attention in grey. (Color figure online)

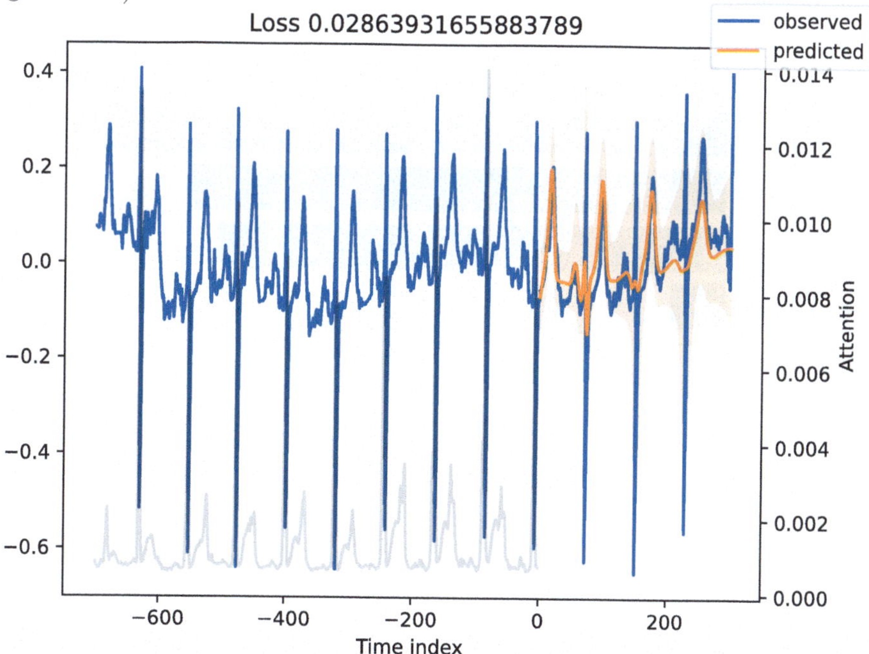

Fig. 4. Predicted (orange) vs. actual Lead 1 ECG (blue), attention in grey. (Color figure online)

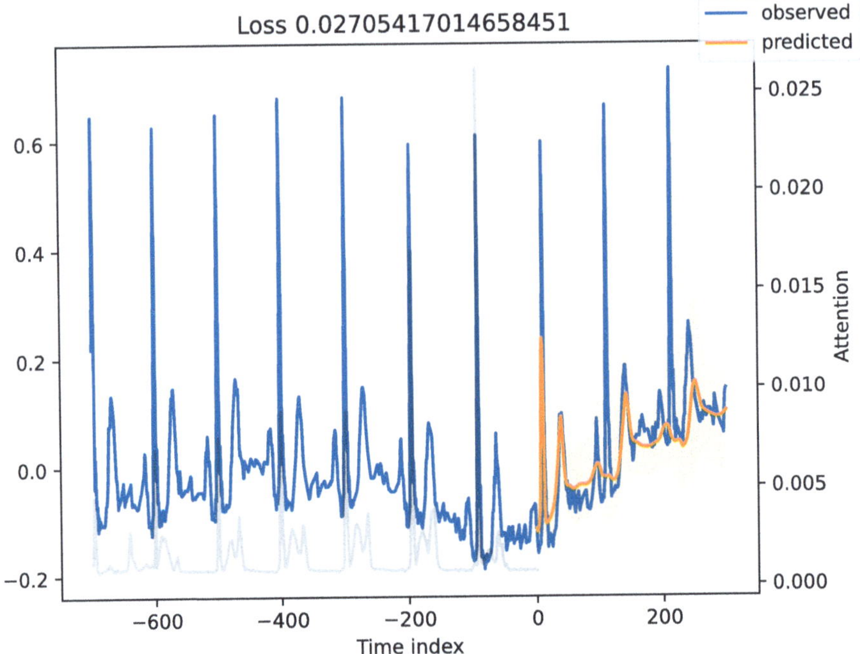

Fig. 5. Predicted (orange) vs. actual Lead 1 ECG (blue), attention in grey. (Color figure online)

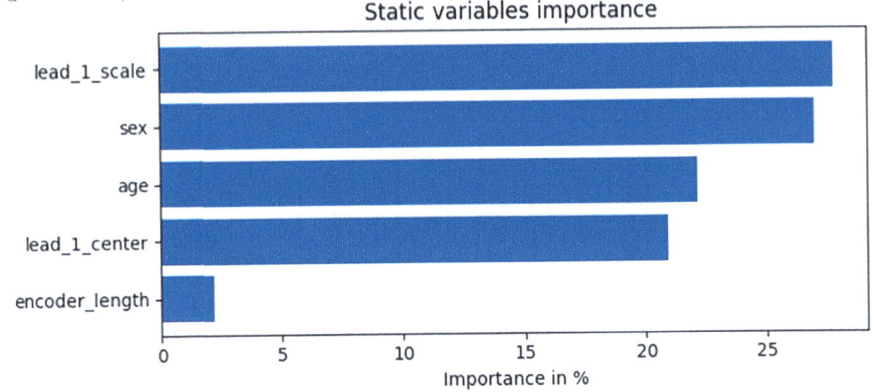

Fig. 6. Variable Importance generated by TFT.

6 Future Work and Conclusion

During this pilot study, we implemented TFT for ECG forecasting - a less explored domain. We were able to predict up to a forecasting window of 300 time steps with good metrics. Since this is a work in progress, many improvements in current work are planned as part of future experiments. As future work, we plan to improve our metrics further by incorporating further domain-specific pre-processing methods and increasing the number of experiments. We plan to cross check the explainability projection of the model with actual medical requirements as part of future work as well.

We also plan to use different feature extraction capabilities as part of static variable input for TFT training.

An optimal forecasting horizon is one of the major goals of this research with respect to the medical requirements. It depends very much on the data history. Therefore long-term ECG data will be used in the near future. As in other application fields, e.g. Financial Time Series Forecasting [7], ECG data can be complex, i.e. non-stationary and chaotic. Therefore further research has already been started on modifications of the TFT and hybrid models incorporating TFTs.

Acknowledgments. The study is sponsored in part by the Bundesministerium fur Bildung und Forschung (BMBF)/German Federal Ministry of Education and Research, Funding program Forschung an Fachhochschulen, KI@FRA-UAS.

Disclosure of Interests. The authors declare that they do not have competing interests.

References

1. Rosa-Bilbao, J., Butt, F.S., Merkl, D., Wagner, M.F., Schäfer, J., Boubeta-Puig, J.: IoT-based indoor air quality management system for intelligent education environments. IEEE Internet Things J. (2025). https://doi.org/10.1109/JIOT.2025.3539886
2. Ratna Prakarsha, K., Sharma, G.: Time series signal forecasting using artificial neural networks: an application on ECG signal. Biomed. Signal Process. Control **76**, 103705 (2022). https://doi.org/10.1016/j.bspc.2022.103705. https://www.sciencedirect.com/science/article/pii/S1746809422002270
3. Hu, X.: Stock price prediction based on temporal fusion transformer. In: Proceedings of the 2021 3rd International Conference on Machine Learning, Big Data and Business Intelligence (MLBDBI), Taiyuan, China, pp. 60–66 (2021). https://doi.org/10.1109/MLBDBI54094.2021.00019
4. Lim, B., Arık, S.Ö., Loeff, N., Pfister, T.: Temporal fusion transformers for interpretable multi-horizon time series forecasting. Int. J. Forecast. **37**(4), 1748–1764 (2021). https://doi.org/10.1016/j.ijforecast.2021.03.012
5. Alharthi, M., Mahmood, A.: xLSTMTime: long-term time series forecasting with xLSTM. AI **5**(3), 1482–1495 (2024)
6. Beck, M., et al.: xLSTM: Extended Long Short-Term Memory, arXiv preprint arXiv:2405.04517 (2024). https://arxiv.org/abs/2405.04517

7. Ho, R., Hung, K.: Ceemd-based multivariate financial time series forecasting using a temporal fusion transformer. In: 2024 IEEE 14th Symposium on Computer Applications & Industrial Electronics (ISCAIE), pp. 209–215. IEEE (2024)
8. Kapral, L., et al.: Development and external validation of temporal fusion transformer models for continuous intraoperative blood pressure forecasting. EClinicalMedicine **75** (2024)
9. Yang, D., et al.: Population-wide depression incidence forecasting comparing autoregressive integrated moving average and vector autoregressive integrated moving average to temporal fusion transformers: longitudinal observational study. J. Med. Internet Res. **27**, e67156 (2025). https://www.jmir.org/2025/1/e67156. https://doi.org/10.2196/67156
10. Lindemann, B., Müller, T., Vietz, H., Jazdi, N., Weyrich, M.: A survey on long short-term memory networks for time series prediction. Procedia CIRP **99**, 650–655 (2021). 14th CIRP Conference on Intelligent Computation in Manufacturing Engineering, 15–17 July 2020. https://doi.org/10.1016/j.procir.2021.03.088
11. Zacarias, H., Marques, J.A.L., Felizardo, V., Pourvahab, M., Garcia, N.M.: ECG forecasting system based on long short-term memory. Bioengineering **11**(1), 89 (2024). https://doi.org/10.3390/bioengineering11010089
12. Phetrittikun, R., Suvirat, K., Na Pattalung, T., Kongkamol, C., Ingviya, T., Chaichulee, S.: Temporal fusion transformer for forecasting vital sign trajectories in intensive care patients. In: Proceedings of 2021 13th Biomedical Engineering International Conference (BMEiCON), pp. 1–5 (2021). https://doi.org/10.1109/BMEiCON53485.2021.9745215
13. Wagner, P., et al.: PTB-XL, a large publicly available electrocardiography dataset. Sci. Data **7**(1), 154 (2020)

Automatic Feature Extraction for ECG Classification Using Signature Methods

Jörg Schäfer(✉), Ahmed Achour, and Fatima Sajid Butt

Frankfurt University of Applied Sciences, Nibelungenplatz. 1, 60318 Frankfurt am Main, Germany
{jschaefer,fatima.butt}@fra-uas.de, ahmed.achour@stud.fra-uas.de

Abstract. Feature extraction is a vital pre-processing step for time series analysis. Signatures from rough path theory have been proposed as an attractive feature extraction method for machine learning in general. In this study, a pilot study on an Electrocardiogram (ECG) Human activity recognition (HAR) dataset is performed. The signatures for a path of ECG signals were calculated and then tested with different basic classifiers like random forest, and a plain neural network. It is observed that using signatures for features improves the classification accuracy from 74% for raw data to 92% using signatures as features.

Keywords: Rough path theory · Signatures · ECG classification · Time Series Analysis

1 Introduction

Time series analysis is a classical theme in the field of signal processing. The electrocardiogram (ECG) signals present an overview of the heart's health and are used widely as the primary tool for evaluation of generic cardiovascular health as well. These ECG signals have been utilized in recent times for a variety of use cases which are beyond human heart such as emotion recognition [1], human activity detection [5], and biometric identification [8].

With the recent advancements in deep learning techniques and the increasing computing capabilities over the past decade, the focus is shifting from the actual model training to pre-training and post-training of models. During the pre-training phase of the model, data must be prepared using distinct automation techniques. After training, the emphasis has shifted from prediction to explainability. Many recent works focus on different pre-training feature extraction techniques like Kalman filters [2], neural ordinary differential equations [3], and wavelets [4] etc. for time series classification.

We present for the first time, to the best of our knowledge, employment of rough path signatures as feature extractors for ECG classification.

J. Schäfer and J. Boubeta-Puig (Eds.): SGSOACS 2025, CCIS 2831, pp. 99–104, 2026.
https://doi.org/10.1007/978-3-032-14816-2_8

The rest of the paper is organized as follows: Sect. 2 provides the readers with background and literature survey. Section 3 describes the experimental set up and tools used for the proposed methodology. Section 4 discusses in detail the obtained results and Sect. 5 provides the conclusion and proposes further future work to continue exploration in this research area.

2 Background and State of the Art

In this section, we provide a little background to the technologies and methodologies used during this study.

Values ordered in time are known as time series. Time series classification is one of the classical and challenging tasks in time series analysis. Let $\mathbf{x} = \{x_1, x_2, \ldots, x_T\}$ be a univariate time series of length T, where each $x_t \in \mathbb{R}$. Similarly, for a multivariate time series, let $\mathbf{x}_t \in \mathbb{R}^d$, so the full series is $\mathbf{x} = \{\mathbf{x}_1, \mathbf{x}_2, \ldots, \mathbf{x}_T\}$. $\mathcal{D} = \{(\mathbf{x}^{(i)}, y^{(i)})\}_{i=1}^{N}$ be a dataset of N labeled time series samples, where $y^{(i)} \in \mathcal{Y} = \{1, 2, \ldots, C\}$ denotes the class label.

The objective of time series classification is to learn a function:

$$f : \mathbb{R}^{T \times d} \to \mathcal{Y}$$

such that:

$$f(\mathbf{x}) = \hat{y}$$

where $\hat{y}$ is the predicted class label for input $\mathbf{x}$, ideally matching the true label y. The goal is to minimize the expected classification error:

$$\mathbb{E}_{(\mathbf{x},y)\sim P(\mathbf{x},y)} \left[\mathbb{I}(f(\mathbf{x}) \neq y)\right]$$

where $\mathbb{I}(\cdot)$ is the indicator function, and $P(\mathbf{x}, y)$ is the joint probability distribution over time series and labels.

Whilst many studies exist in the literature to extract features carefully to improve the performance of the classifier for time series, application of signature is still a less explored field.

We recall the definition of the signature S as iterated integrals from [12]:

Definition 1 *(Signature). The signature of S a path $\gamma : [s,t] \to \mathbb{R}^d$, denoted by $S(\gamma)_{s,t}$ is the collection (infinite series) of all the iterated integrals of γ. Formally, $S(\gamma)_{s,t}$ is the sequence of real numbers S^N, where*

$$S^N(X)_{s,t} := \left(1, \int_{s<u<t} dx_u, \ldots, \int_{s<u_1<\ldots<u_k<t} dx_{u_1} \otimes \ldots \otimes dx_{u_k}\right) \in \bigoplus_{k=0}^{N} (\mathbb{R}^d)^{\otimes^k}$$

and the superscripts run along the set of all multi-indexes $W = \{(i_1, \ldots, i_k) \mid k \geq 1, i_1, \ldots, i_k \in \{1, ..., d\}\}$. This implies that $S \in \bigoplus_{k=0}^{\infty} (\mathbb{R}^d)^{\otimes^k}$. The set W above is also frequently called the set of words on the alphabet $A = 1, \ldots, d$ consisting of d letters.

The usefulness of signatures for feature extraction stems from the well-known universal non-linearity theorem [6]:

Theorem 1 *(Universal non-linearity). Let F be a real-valued continuous function on continuous piecewise smooth paths in* $\mathbb{R}^d$ *and let K be a compact set of such paths. Furthermore assume that* $X_0 = 0$ *for all* $X \in K$. *(To remove the translation invariance.) Let* $\epsilon > 0$. *Then there exists a linear functional L such that for all* $X \in K$, $||F(X) - L(S(X)|| < \epsilon$.

According to Chevyrev et al. [10], signatures have many useful mathematical properties like invariance under time reparameterization and shuffle product etc. Lyons et al. [6] presented a comprehensive report describing application of signatures in machine learning. Yang et al. [9] used signature path for landmark human activity recognition classification and improved the accuracy over other state-of-the-art methods. Sun et al. [11] used signature paths to classify network time series in an explainable way by proposing a signature based deep learning neural network.

3 Experimental Set Up and Methodology

The dataset used in this study is a single-lead ECG dataset designed for human activity recognition, including fall detection [13]. It comprises three labeled classes: fall, rest, and daily activities as shown in Fig. 1.

The idea to use an appropriate feature extractor to increase the classification capability is derived mainly from our previous studies, [4,5], in which we used wavelets and feature maps as feature extractors on different datasets. All experiments for this study were carried out on a high computing GPU NVIDIA A100 GPU. The Python library *iisignatures* designed by Reizenstein et al. [7] was used to calculate the signatures at a given level for each of the input readings. All experiments were performed using the PyTorch framework.

After reading the raw values, standard time embedding was added as the first coordinate for signature calculation. The raw values are normalized [0, 1] for numerical stability in signature calculation. After the signatures were calculated, the experiments were performed initially on the raw signatures and later on recombined signatures. For raw signatures, all levels are concatenated together and levels are not separated. However, we separate signatures level wise in second phase of calculating signatures which we call 'recombined signature'. We make sure that for a signature of level l, the output signal should have total tuples of l signatures each for each level. After calculating the signatures, they were scaled with $l!$ as signatures scale $1/l!$ and we require features of the same order of magnitude. After calculating the signatures, the signatures are fed into different classifiers to evaluate their results. The raw dataset before the signature transformation was also fed into classifiers to form a baseline result. As we try to calculate higher levels of signatures, the required computational power increases.

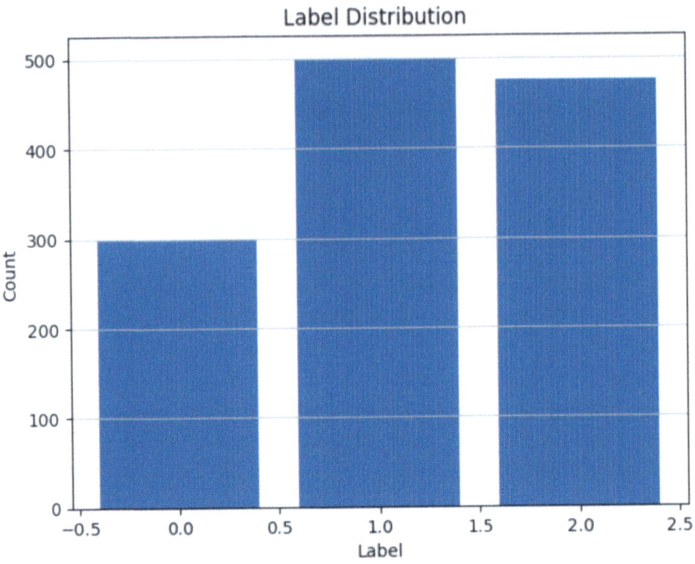

Fig. 1. The overview of data points in each of the label class for the HAR dataset.

4 Results and Discussion

The Random forest produces an accuracy of 0.749 and 0.4156 on support vector machine on raw data respectively. The results after calculating different signature levels are shown in Table 1.

Table 1. Model performance in accuracy at various signature levels using different classifiers. RF = Random forest, SVM = Support Vector Machines, NN = Neural Network

Signature level	RF	SVM	NN
Raw signatures			
5	0.852	0.647	0.76
10	0.906	0.4	0.839
15	0.914	0.843	
Comb and recombined signatures			
10	0.922	0.796	0.87
15	0.922	0.843	0.906

The metric chosen was accuracy and confusion matrix to visualize the classification. It can be seen that accuracy increases with the increase in signature level up to a certain level in general.

The best results for both raw and recombine signatures are achieved by simple random forest. A plain neural network with multiple layers still did not outperform random forest. Support vector machines start to perform better at higher level signatures. However for lower levels, they do not classify it all.

5 Conclusion and Future Work

In this pilot study, we used signatures from rough path theory as feature extractor for classifiers. The results show significant improvement in classification accuracy with using higher level signatures. However, they still do not achieve state of the art accuracy for the given dataset. This provides us the basis for future experiments.

For future work, we plan to work towards improving the accuracy by reorganizing the signatures after calculating to maintain the hierarchical structure. We also plan to experiment with more deep learning classifiers like transformers and LSTMs.

Acknowledgments. The study is sponsored in part by the Bundesministerium fur Bildung und Forschung (BMBF)/German Federal Ministry of Education and Research, Funding program Forschung an Fachhochschulen, KI@FRA-UAS.

Disclosure of Interests. The authors declare that they do not have competing interests.

References

1. Hasnul, M.A., Aziz, N.A.A., Alelyani, S., Mohana, M., Aziz, A.A.: Electrocardiogram-based emotion recognition systems and their applications in healthcare-a review. Sensors (Basel) **21**(15), 5015 (2021). https://doi.org/10.3390/s21155015
2. Tang, H., et al.: Feature extraction of multi-sensors for early bearing fault diagnosis using deep learning based on minimum unscented Kalman filter. Eng. Appl. Artif. Intell. **127**, 107138 (2024). https://doi.org/10.1016/j.engappai.2023.107138
3. Jhin, S.Y., et al.: Attentive neural controlled differential equations for time-series classification and forecasting. Knowl. Inf. Syst. **66**(3), 1885–1915 (2024). https://doi.org/10.1007/s10115-023-01977-5
4. Butt, F.S., Wagner, M.F., Schäfer, J., Ullate, D.G.: Toward automated feature extraction for deep learning classification of electrocardiogram signals. IEEE Access **10**, 118601–118616 (2022). https://doi.org/10.1109/ACCESS.2022.3207479
5. Butt, F.S., La Blunda, L., Wagner, M.F., Schäfer, J., Medina-Bulo, I., Gómez-Ullate, D.: Fall detection from electrocardiogram (ECG) signals and classification by deep transfer learning. Information **12**(2), 63 (2021). https://doi.org/10.3390/info12020063
6. Lyons, T., McLeod, A.D.: Signature methods in machine learning (2025). arXiv preprint arXiv:2206.14674
7. Jeremy, F.R., Benjamin, G.: Algorithm 1004: The iisignature library: efficient calculation of iterated-integral signatures and log signatures. ACM Trans. Math. Softw. **46**(1), 21, p. 8 (2020). https://doi.org/10.1145/3371237

8. Guven, G., Gürkan, H., Guz, U.: Biometric identification using fingertip electrocardiogram signals. SIViP **12**(5), 933–940 (2018). https://doi.org/10.1007/s11760-018-1238-4
9. Yang, W., Lyons, T., Ni, H., Schmid, C., Jin, L.: Developing the path signature methodology and its application to landmark-based human action recognition. In: Yin, G., Zariphopoulou, T. (eds.) Stochastic Analysis, Filtering, and Stochastic Optimization: A Commemorative Volume to Honor Mark H. A. Davis's Contributions, pp. 431–464. Springer International Publishing, Cham (2022). https://doi.org/10.1007/978-3-030-98519-6_18
10. Chevyrev, I., Kormilitzin, A.: A primer on the signature method in machine learning (2025). arXiv preprint arXiv:1603.03788
11. Sun, L., Wang, Y., Ren, Y., Xia, F.: Path signature-based XAI-enabled network time series classification. Sci. China Inf. Sci. **67**(7), 170305 (2024). https://doi.org/10.1007/s11432-023-3978-y
12. Friz, P.K., Victoir, N.B.: Multidimensional Stochastic Processes as Rough Paths: Theory and Applications. Cambridge Studies in Advanced Mathematics. Cambridge University Press (2010)
13. Butt, F.S., La Blunda, L., Wagner, M.F., Schäfer, J., Medina-Bulo, I., Gómez-Ullate Oteiza, D.: ECG data for deep transfer learning. IEEE Dataport (2020). https://doi.org/10.3390/info12020063

Security

Enabling Cross-Platform Blockchain Integration in Low-Code Development: Extending EDALoCo with Hyperledger Firefly

Jesús Rosa-Bilbao[1(✉)], Guzmán Llambías[2], Juan Boubeta-Puig[1], and Laura González[2]

[1] UCASE Software Engineering Research Group, Department of Computer Science and Engineering, University of Cadiz, Avda. de la Universidad de Cádiz 10, 11519 Puerto Real, Cádiz, Spain
jesus.rosa@uca.es, juan.boubeta@uca.es

[2] Universidad de la República, J. H. Reissig 565, 11300 Montevideo, Uruguay
gllambi@fing.edu.uy, lauragon@fing.edu.uy

Abstract. Enterprise Blockchain-Based Applications (EBBA) require seamless interaction with diverse blockchain platforms to address the growing heterogeneity of enterprise ecosystems. Traditional development approaches demand deep expertise in blockchain-specific technologies, significantly increasing development complexity, time, and costs. The EDALoCo low-code platform was initially designed to facilitate EBBA development by abstracting the complexities of Ethereum Virtual Machine (EVM)-based blockchains. However, its initial scope limited interoperability, preventing integration with non-EVM networks critical to many enterprise scenarios. This work presents the extension of EDALoCo to enable cross-platform blockchain integration by incorporating Hyperledger Firefly as a middleware abstraction layer. Two new low-code components were developed to support event subscription and smart contract interaction with non-EVM blockchains, substantially enhancing EDALoCo's versatility. A prototype was implemented and validated using Hyperledger Fabric as the target non-EVM blockchain. The results demonstrate that extending low-code platforms with cross-blockchain capabilities is technically feasible and highly beneficial, paving the way for blockchain-agnostic enterprise solutions that lower development barriers while embracing network heterogeneity.

Keywords: Blockchain · Low-code · Ethereum Virtual Machine · Hyperledger Firefly · Interoperability

1 Introduction

Blockchain technology is increasingly being adopted across various industries, giving rise to a heterogeneous ecosystem of blockchain platforms [2,8]. Enterprise Blockchain-Based Applications (EBBA) must often interact with multiple

J. Schäfer and J. Boubeta-Puig (Eds.): SGSOACS 2025, CCIS 2831, pp. 107–116, 2026.
https://doi.org/10.1007/978-3-032-14816-2_9

blockchain technologies, each with distinct architectures, consensus mechanisms, and interfaces. This poses significant challenges for software developers, as developing and maintaining multi-chain applications requires specialized expertise and extensive resources.

To mitigate these challenges, low-code development platforms have emerged as a promising solution [6], enabling developers with limited blockchain expertise to design, deploy, and manage blockchain-integrated applications. EDALoCo is one such platform, originally designed to simplify the development of event-driven blockchain applications targeting Ethereum Virtual Machine (EVM)-based blockchains.

In a previous work [11], we proposed a gateway-based interoperability solution that enables interoperability between EVM-based blockchains and non-EVM blockchains. However, the approach is low-level and follows a request-response interaction in contrast with the low-level and event-driven approach of the EDALoCo platform.

On the other hand, the initial version of EDALoCo restricted application development to EVM-compatible environments, limiting its applicability in multi-chain enterprise scenarios. Addressing this limitation, this work proposes an extension of EDALoCo that introduces support for cross-platform blockchain integration through Hyperledger Firefly, enabling communication with both EVM and non-EVM-based blockchains such as Hyperledger Fabric [1].

By enhancing EDALoCo's interoperability capabilities, this research contributes to bridging the gap between heterogeneous blockchain platforms within enterprise ecosystems [18], promoting more flexible and blockchain-agnostic application development [16]. The prototype implementation and validation offer insights into the technical feasibility and potential benefits of this approach. Please note that a brief version of this work was published as an extended abstract in [10].

The remainder of this paper is structured as follows: Sect. 2 presents the background of the proposal. Section 3 reviews related work on blockchain interoperability and low-code development. Section 4 describes the architecture and implementation of the EDALoCo extensions. Finally, Sect. 5 concludes the paper and outlines directions for future work.

2 Background

To provide a comprehensive understanding of the challenges and motivations behind this work, this section reviews the essential concepts related to EBBA, the role and importance of blockchain interoperability, and the potential of low-code development platforms in facilitating blockchain integration.

2.1 Enterprise Blockchain-Based Applications

EBBAs leverage blockchain technology to improve efficiency, transparency, and security within enterprise business processes [14]. Unlike public blockchain applications, EBBA often operate in permissioned environments, where access and participation are restricted to authorized entities. Typical enterprise use cases include supply chain management, financial services, healthcare data sharing, and inter-organizational workflows [17].

Despite their potential, the development of EBBA remains challenging. Developers must navigate complex blockchain-specific concepts such as smart contracts, consensus protocols, on-chain/off-chain data management, and identity management systems. Furthermore, integrating blockchain components with existing enterprise IT infrastructures—often legacy systems—adds another layer of complexity. These technical hurdles not only slow down development cycles but also increase the required investment in specialized skills and training [3].

As enterprise environments increasingly adopt multi-chain strategies to avoid vendor lock-in and leverage diverse blockchain features, the demand for flexible, interoperable solutions has intensified. Addressing these challenges necessitates new approaches that simplify blockchain integration while maintaining the robustness required by enterprise applications.

2.2 Blockchain Interoperability

Blockchain interoperability refers to the ability of different blockchain networks to communicate, share data, and facilitate transactions across their distinct infrastructures [9]. In the context of enterprise applications, interoperability is essential for enabling cross-organizational collaboration, supporting multi-chain business processes, and achieving scalability without compromising decentralization.

Several factors complicate interoperability, including differences in consensus algorithms, data models, smart contract languages, and governance structures [13]. Without interoperability mechanisms, blockchain ecosystems risk becoming isolated silos, undermining the vision of a connected decentralized world.

Various interoperability solutions have emerged, ranging from sidechains (e.g., Polygon PoS) and blockchain of blockchains models (e.g., Cosmos, Polkadot) to middleware platforms like Hyperledger Firefly that abstract blockchain interactions through standardized APIs. For enterprise scenarios, where reliability, auditability, and performance are critical, middleware-based interoperability approaches offer a promising path by providing a unified layer that connects disparate blockchains while preserving their autonomy.

2.3 Low-Code Development Platforms

Low-Code Development Platforms (LCDP) aim to simplify the creation of complex software applications by minimizing the amount of manual coding required. They offer visual programming interfaces, prebuilt components, and integration templates, enabling users—including those with limited programming experience—to rapidly develop and deploy applications.

In the context of blockchain application development, low-code platforms present a significant opportunity [6]. They can abstract blockchain-specific complexities such as smart contract deployment, event listening, transaction management, and identity handling. By lowering technical barriers, low-code platforms democratize access to blockchain technology, foster innovation, and accelerate time-to-market for enterprise applications.

However, existing low-code blockchain platforms have often focused on a single blockchain technology, particularly EVM-compatible networks. This narrow focus limits their applicability in heterogeneous enterprise environments that increasingly require multi-chain interoperability. Extending low-code platforms to support cross-blockchain development is therefore a crucial step toward mainstream enterprise blockchain adoption.

3 Related Work

To contextualize the contributions of this work, this section reviews existing efforts related to blockchain interoperability and low-code development platforms. We analyze prominent interoperability solutions and identify the limitations of current low-code approaches for enterprise blockchain application development.

3.1 Interoperability Solutions

Blockchain interoperability has become a critical research topic as the number of blockchain networks and enterprise use cases continues to grow. Several projects have emerged to address the interoperability challenge through different architectural approaches.

Polkadot introduces a relay-chain model that connects multiple heterogeneous blockchains allowing them to communicate securely through shared consensus mechanisms [15]. Similarly, Cosmos employs a hub-and-spoke model through the Inter-Blockchain Communication (IBC) protocol, enabling independent blockchains to transfer assets and data seamlessly [4].

For enterprise contexts, middleware platforms such as Hyperledger Firefly [7] offer a different perspective by abstracting blockchain-specific interactions through unified APIs. This approach simplifies integration across diverse blockchain networks, making it particularly attractive for low-code and event-driven application development.

Other notable initiatives, including Wanchain and Chainlink, propose cross-chain solutions but primarily target asset interoperability or are limited to EVM-based blockchains. Enterprise solutions often require broader data and transaction interoperability beyond token transfers and EVM-based blockchains such as Hyperledger Fabric.

3.2 Low-Code Approaches in Blockchain Development

Low-code development paradigms have been applied to blockchain environments to lower entry barriers and accelerate application delivery. EDALoCo [12] stands out as a pioneering initiative aiming to simplify the creation of blockchain-based event-driven applications through a user-friendly visual environment.

Other frameworks such as SIMBA Chain [5] provide low-code APIs and smart contract templates for blockchain application development, although their interoperability capabilities remain limited to specific platforms like Ethereum and Hyperledger Fabric.

Despite these advancements, existing low-code solutions typically focus on isolated blockchain ecosystems. A critical need remains for low-code platforms that can seamlessly support cross-blockchain interactions, fostering true interoperability in enterprise blockchain applications.

4 Extending EDALoCo for Cross-Blockchain Integration

This section introduces the architectural and functional evolution of EDALoCo to support cross-blockchain interoperability. We begin by analyzing the limitations of the original platform, followed by the presentation of the updated architecture designed to decouple EDALoCo from blockchain-specific constraints. We then describe the integration strategy using Hyperledger Firefly as a middleware layer, and conclude by detailing the new low-code components that operationalize multi-chain interaction.

4.1 Limitations of the Original EDALoCo Design

EDALoCo was initially developed to simplify the construction of blockchain-based enterprise applications on EVM-compatible networks. Through a low-code approach, it abstracted much of the complexity related to smart contract deployment, invocation, and event handling. While effective within its original scope, the platform exhibited several limitations that hindered its applicability in emerging enterprise blockchain scenarios:

- **EVM Dependence:** EDALoCo was confined to EVM-compatible chains such as Ethereum, Binance Smart Chain, or Polygon, excluding platforms like Hyperledger Fabric, Corda, or Quorum.
- **Lack of Cross-Chain Capabilities:** Applications were restricted to a single blockchain environment, limiting integration in hybrid or federated enterprise settings.
- **Scalability and Adaptability Issues:** Extending the platform to new blockchain technologies required intrusive architectural changes, making EDALoCo less agile in responding to rapid blockchain innovation.

These constraints motivated the design of a more flexible and modular architecture capable of supporting heterogeneous multi-chain deployments.

4.2 Proposed Architecture and Integration Strategy

The updated EDALoCo architecture introduces a middleware layer to abstract blockchain-specific operations, thus enabling communication with both EVM and non-EVM networks. The goal is to retain EDALoCo's low-code philosophy while making the platform adaptable to hybrid enterprise ecosystems.

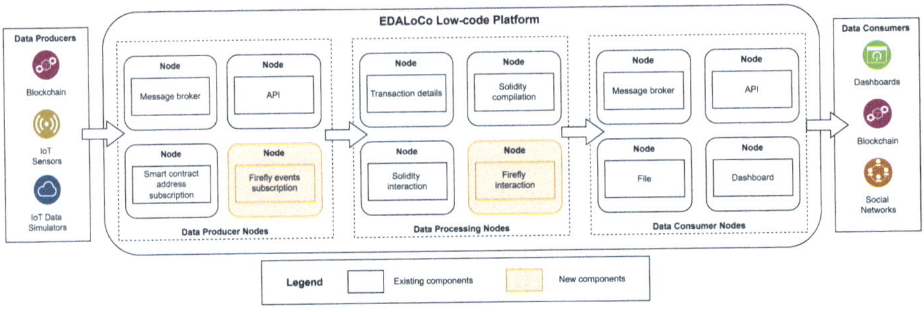

Fig. 1. EDALoCo low-code platform extensions enabling cross-blockchain interoperability (extracted from [10]).

As shown in Fig. 1, the updated architecture introduces a modular integration layer between the low-code workflow engine and the blockchain networks. This layer is responsible for managing contract execution, event flow, and data synchronization across chains. The core elements of the architecture are:

- **Low-code interface:** The user-facing component remains unchanged, preserving the graphical programming environment of EDALoCo.
- **Middleware abstraction layer:** This decouples EDALoCo's internal logic from the specifics of blockchain protocols.
- **Blockchain connectors:** Each supported blockchain network (EVM or non-EVM) is linked via the middleware's pluggable connectors.

This modularity allows EDALoCo to support dynamic reconfiguration and scaling in multi-chain enterprise environments.

Although this work employs Hyperledger Firefly as the middleware abstraction layer, the proposed architecture is not inherently tied to Firefly's specific APIs. The integration layer is modular by design, enabling the substitution or coexistence of other middleware platforms that expose equivalent contract invocation and event subscription interfaces. For example, future iterations could support Cosmos IBC gateways or bespoke enterprise interoperability engines, provided they offer standard or easily adaptable APIs. This architectural flexibility ensures that EDALoCo remains extensible and resilient to changes in middleware ecosystems, thereby promoting long-term sustainability and broader applicability.

4.3 Middleware-Based Integration Using Hyperledger Firefly

To implement the abstraction layer defined in the architecture, we integrated Hyperledger Firefly, a Web3 middleware designed for enterprise-grade blockchain solutions. Firefly simplifies and unifies interactions with diverse blockchain backends through a set of standardized REST APIs. Key features of Firefly that enable this integration include:

- **Smart Contract Interaction:** Firefly provides an API layer to invoke smart contracts on any supported blockchain. This abstracts protocol-specific transaction logic, allowing EDALoCo to trigger contract execution uniformly across networks.
- **Event Subscription and Processing:** Firefly supports real-time event monitoring across chains. Events are normalized and delivered through its event stream mechanism, which can be consumed by EDALoCo to drive workflows.
- **Identity Management:** Enterprise identity resolution is handled internally by Firefly, reducing the need for EDALoCo to manage decentralized identities directly.
- **Off-Chain Data Orchestration:** Firefly includes components for off-chain data broadcasting, pinning, and message exchange—key features for hybrid applications that blend on-chain and off-chain logic.

The use of Firefly transforms EDALoCo into a chain-agnostic platform. Developers continue working within the same low-code environment, while Firefly manages the translation and execution of blockchain operations behind the scenes.

4.4 New Low-Code Components for Multi-chain Interaction

To make the middleware capabilities available within EDALoCo's visual programming environment, two new low-code nodes were introduced:

- **Firefly Interaction Node:** This node abstracts contract invocation. Developers configure the contract interface, select methods, and provide parameters via a user-friendly form. Internally, the node composes a REST API call to Firefly, which executes the transaction on the appropriate blockchain.
- **Firefly Event Subscription Node:** This node allows EDALoCo to listen for and respond to blockchain events. Developers can define filters for event types, contracts, and topics. When Firefly detects a matching event, it forwards it to this node, which then activates the corresponding workflow in EDALoCo.

Both nodes are designed to align with EDALoCo's principles of accessibility and usability. They enable developers to build multi-chain, event-driven applications without needing to write code or understand the nuances of different blockchain platforms.

4.5 Security Considerations and Trust Assumptions

The integration of a middleware abstraction layer such as Hyperledger Firefly introduces a new trust boundary into the EDALoCo architecture. While the middleware simplifies cross-platform interaction and abstracts blockchain-specific complexities, it also consolidates the control and flow of blockchain operations, becoming a critical component of the system's trust model.

In this architecture, Firefly is assumed to operate in a semi-trusted environment. It provides authentication, access control, and message integrity mechanisms to secure interactions with blockchain networks. All communications between EDALoCo and Firefly are conducted over HTTPS, and Firefly's internal identity resolution mechanisms enforce access boundaries based on organization-level identities.

Although this design reduces the need for developers to directly manage credentials or transaction signing logic, it centralizes operational responsibility within the middleware layer. Consequently, securing the Firefly deployment—including API access controls, logging, and runtime isolation—is essential to maintaining the integrity and confidentiality of cross-chain workflows.

The middleware layer thus represents both an enabler of interoperability and a potential attack surface, requiring careful configuration and monitoring. The EDALoCo platform delegates blockchain-specific trust assumptions (e.g., consensus and permissioning) to the underlying networks while relying on the middleware to enforce protocol-agnostic guarantees on top of them.

5 Conclusions and Future Work

This work has proposed the extension of EDALoCo, a low-code platform originally designed for EVM-based blockchain applications, to enable cross-blockchain interoperability through the integration of Hyperledger Firefly. By decoupling application logic from specific blockchain technologies, the platform now allows enterprise developers to seamlessly interact with both EVM and non-EVM blockchains within a unified development environment.

The introduction of new low-code components —Firefly Interaction and Firefly Event Subscription nodes— significantly enhances EDALoCo's versatility, aligning it with the growing need for blockchain-agnostic enterprise solutions. This advancement reduces technical barriers, minimizes vendor lock-in risks, and accelerates the development of complex, multi-chain applications.

Despite these benefits, challenges remain. Middleware-based integration introduces performance overheads and new security considerations. Additionally, coordinating cross-chain transactions and achieving standardized interoperability protocols continue to be open research areas. Addressing these issues will be crucial to realizing the full potential of low-code platforms in heterogeneous blockchain ecosystems.

Future work will focus on expanding EDALoCo's support for additional blockchain platforms such as Corda and Tezos, as well as developing abstractions for smart contract interoperability and exploring mechanisms for seamless multi-chain transaction orchestration. To optimize the platform's scalability and reliability, systematic performance benchmarking will be conducted, including the evaluation of key indicators such as transaction latency, throughput, and event processing time across both EVM and non-EVM networks mediated through Firefly. Furthermore, user studies involving developers with varying levels of blockchain expertise will be carried out to assess the usability and learning curve of the new low-code components. These empirical evaluations will provide a stronger foundation for the platform's claims regarding accessibility, efficiency, and its suitability for multi-chain enterprise scenarios.

By pursuing these future research lines, EDALoCo will able to evolve into a pioneering platform at the intersection of low-code development and blockchain interoperability, driving broader adoption and innovation in enterprise blockchain solutions.

Acknowledgments. This publication is part of the I+D+i grant PID2021-122215NB-C33 funded by MICIU/AEI/10.13039/501100011033 and by ERDF/EU. Guzmán Llambías was supported by Pyxis. The research that gives rise to the results presented in this publication received funds from the Agencia Nacional de Investigación e Innovación under the code POS_NAC_2022_4_174476.

Disclosure of Interests. The authors have no competing interests to declare that are relevant to the content of this article.

References

1. Androulaki, E., et al.: Hyperledger fabric: a distributed operating system for permissioned blockchains. In: Proceedings of the Thirteenth EuroSys Conference, pp. 1–15. ACM (2018). https://doi.org/10.1145/3190508.3190538
2. Belchior, R., Vasconcelos, A., Guerreiro, S., Correia, M.: A survey on blockchain interoperability: past, present, and future trends. ACM Comput. Surv. **54**(8), 1–41 (2022). https://doi.org/10.1145/3471140
3. Boubeta-Puig, J., Rosa-Bilbao, J., Mendling, J.: CEPchain: a graphical model-driven solution for integrating complex event processing and blockchain. Exp. Syst. Appl. **184**, 115578 (2021). https://doi.org/10.1016/j.eswa.2021.115578
4. Buchman, E., Kwon, J., Milosevic, Z.: Cosmos (2020). https://cosmos.network/. Accessed 27 Apr 2025
5. SIMBA Chain: SIMBA Chain Platform Overview (2024). https://simbachain.com. Accessed 27 Apr 2025
6. Curty, S., Härer, F., Fill, H.G.: Design of blockchain-based applications using model-driven engineering and low-code/no-code platforms: a structured literature review. Softw. Syst. Model. **22**, 1857–1895 (2023). https://doi.org/10.1007/s10270-023-01109-1
7. Foundation, H.: Hyperledger Firefly Documentation (2024). https://hyperledger.github.io/firefly/latest/. Accessed 27 Apr 2025
8. Liu, Y., Zhang, Y., Wang, J., et al.: Technologies of blockchain interoperability: a survey. Digit. Commun. Netw. **11**(1), 210–224 (2025). https://doi.org/10.1016/j.dcan.2023.07.008

9. Llambías, G., González, L., Ruggia, R.: Blockchain interoperability: a feature-based classification framework and challenges ahead. CLEI Electron. J. **25**(3), 4–1 (2022). https://doi.org/10.19153/cleiej.25.3.4
10. Llambías, G., Rosa-Bilbao, J., Boubeta-Puig, J., González, L.: Extending EDALoCo to support the development of enterprise blockchain-based applications following a low-code approach. In: Actas de las Jornadas Uruguayas de Ciencias de la Computación 2024 Jorge Vidart, pp. 35–37. Udelar. FI. INCO: CES, Montevideo (2025)
11. Pandolfi, S., González, E., Castro, M., Llambías, G., González, L., Ruggia, R.: Interoperability between DLT following a gateway-based approach: the case of ethereum and hyperledger fabric. In: 2023 XLIX Latin American Computer Conference (CLEI), La Paz, Bolivia, October 2023, pp. 1–10 (2023). https://doi.org/10.1109/CLEI60451.2023.10346168
12. Rosa-Bilbao, J., Boubeta-Puig, J., Rutle, A.: EDALoCo: enhancing the accessibility of blockchains through a low-code approach to the development of event-driven applications for smart contract management. Comput. Stan. Interfaces **84**, 103676 (2023). https://doi.org/10.1016/j.csi.2022.103676
13. Smith, J., Doe, J.: Blockchain interoperability: the state of heterogeneous blockchain systems. IET Commun. **17**(3), 245–256 (2023). https://doi.org/10.1049/cmu2.12594
14. Sunny, F.A., Hajek, P., Munk, M., Abedin, M.Z., Satu, M.S., Efat, M.I.A., Islam, M.J.: A systematic review of blockchain applications. IEEE Access **10**, 59155–59177 (2022). https://doi.org/10.1109/ACCESS.2022.3179690
15. Wood, G., et al.: Polkadot (2020). https://polkadot.com/. Accessed 27 Apr 2025
16. Yan, Y.: IEEE standard for blockchain interoperability data authentication and communication protocol. IEEE Std 3205-2023, pp. 1–37 (2023). https://doi.org/10.1109/IEEESTD.2023.10108929
17. Zhang, W., Li, M., Zhao, L.: Blockchain Technology, Enterprise Risk and Enterprise Performance. Sustainability **16**(1), 70 (2024). https://doi.org/10.3390/su16010070
18. Zhang, W., Li, M., Zhao, L., et al.: A survey on privacy preservation techniques for blockchain interoperability. J. Syst. Architect. **140**, 102892 (2023). https://doi.org/10.1016/j.sysarc.2023.102892

Implementation of a Framework for Early Anomaly Detection in Naval Systems

Manuel Suano-Gallardo[1(✉)], Rafael Gómez Sánchez[2], Sara Balderas-Díaz[1], Gabriel Guerrero-Contreras[1], and Inmaculada Medina-Bulo[1]

[1] Department of Computer Science and Engineering, University of Cadiz, Av. Universidad de Cádiz, 10, 11519 Puerto Real, Cádiz, Spain
{manuel.suano,sara.balderas,gabriel.guerrero,inmaculada.medina}@uca.es

[2] Navantia Sistemas, Ctra de la Carraca s/n, 11100 San Fernando (Cádiz), Spain
rgomezsa@navantia.es

Abstract. The rapid digital transformation and the ongoing paradigm shift towards Industry 4.0 have significantly augmented interconnectivity through the integration of sophisticated technologies within industrial networks, server infrastructure, and cloud environments. Consequently, these interconnected systems are increasingly susceptible to critical security vulnerabilities, including illicit access to confidential information and acts of sabotage. Recognizing the limitations of existing security systems, including intrusion detection systems and security information and event management systems, in addressing novel threats, we propose complex event processing (CEP) as an effective countermeasure. CEP enables the timely and real-time detection of cyberattacks within operational technology (OT) and the Internet of Things (IoT) environments, exhibiting adaptability to the resource constraints of these devices. This work presents a framework of a specific architecture tailored for OT and IoT, implementing CEP on Advanced RISC Machine (ARM) devices to improve the early identification of cyber intrusions, including its human-machine interface (HMI). The proposed framework operates by capturing network traffic and processing it through a CEP engine to automatically identify anomalous patterns. The framework's efficacy is validated through its integration into Navantia's integrated bridge system within a real-world deployment.

Keywords: Cybersecurity · Industry 4.0 · Internet of Things · Complex Event Processing · Operational Technology · Anomaly Detection

1 Introduction

The increasing hyperconnectivity of Industry 4.0, driven by new technologies and vast amounts of data, introduces significant cybersecurity challenges, particularly for industrial systems that were not initially designed for internet connectivity

J. Schäfer and J. Boubeta-Puig (Eds.): SGSOACS 2025, CCIS 2831, pp. 117–131, 2026.
https://doi.org/10.1007/978-3-032-14816-2_10

[13]. This vulnerability has led to an increase in attacks on critical infrastructures, aiming to steal data or sabotage operations. Current Information Technology (IT) centric security solutions like intrusion detection systems (IDS) and security information and event management (SIEM) have limitations in detecting novel threats and compatibility with operational technology/Internet of Things environments [4,12].

Complex event processing [10] is emerging as a key technology for real-time analysis of large data volumes to detect cybersecurity events. Although machine learning for anomaly detection in IoT is growing, it can suffer from false positives [3].

In a previous work, we presented an architecture that combines the efficiency of CEP in resource-constrained environments with the adaptability of machine learning for real-time anomaly detection across IT, OT, and IoT systems [5]. That work represented the initial phase of the ongoing SEADETEC project. A project in collaboration with Navantia (running from June 2023 to June 2026) under INCIBE's Strategic Initiative for Innovative Public Procurement aims to develop key cybersecurity products through joint research and development with major industrial players [7].

This paper presents the second phase of the SEADETEC project, which focuses on the implementation of a framework based on the proposed architecture, incorporating a human-machine interface tailored to OT/IoT environments. While [5] laid the theoretical groundwork and proposed the architecture, this current work presents a framework that implements that architecture and the integration of an HMI specifically designed for OT/IoT interaction, addressing the practical deployment challenges.

The rest of this paper is structured as follows: Sect. 2 details the state of the art. Section 3 presents the proposed framework including its architecture and its HMI. Finally, Sect. 4 summarizes the conclusions and future work.

2 State of the Art

The ongoing paradigm shift towards Industry 4.0 is driving massive global investment in interconnected systems, projected to reach €156.6 trillion by 2024 with a 16% annual growth [8]. This hyperconnectivity, however, intensifies cybersecurity risks, particularly for industrial control systems, which are increasingly targeted by ransomware and data theft [2,14]. Operational disruptions from cyberattacks can severely impact core business functions. Consequently, robust and integrated cybersecurity, spanning from plant management to field operations and intellectual property, is now a critical strategic imperative for all businesses.

Historically, industrial security focused on physical safety. However, Industry 4.0's reliance on virtual technologies necessitates a shift towards comprehensive cybersecurity to secure facilities, data integrity, and confidential production information. Industrial cybersecurity must address both physical and virtual threats, which are often interconnected. Recognizing this, national cybersecurity strategies are prioritizing cyberspace security.

Current IT-centric security solutions like rule-based IDS struggle to detect novel attacks and require expert configuration. SIEM systems demand significant hardware and lack compatibility with resource-constrained IoT/OT environments. To overcome these limitations and enable early detection in IoT, complex event processing is a key technology for real-time analysis of large datasets [11]. While machine learning for anomaly detection in IoT is growing, it can produce many false positives, especially in complex scenarios [1,6,9].

Addressing this gap, there is a need for intuitive software solutions that automatically detect both known attacks and anomalies in IT/OT/IoT environments in real time, even with limited resources and for users without expert knowledge. Previous work has explored integrating CEP and machine learning for early detection in non-industrial IoT [11]. This project builds on that experience to apply this integration to the IT/OT and industrial IoT environment of Navantia, in particular, the MINERVA integrated bridge system, aiming for successful implementation.

3 The Proposed Framework

3.1 Architecture

Figure 1 illustrates our architecture of the SEADETEC system presented in [5].

The architecture efficiently processes sensor data from the monitored system. Initially, information from various sensors undergoes filtering and transformation into JSON format. This standardised data is then published to a messaging broker.

A key component of this architecture is the complex event processing engine, which acts as a consumer for the messaging broker. SEADETEC, for instance, integrates a CEP engine, specifically Esper version 9.0, for real-time data analysis within OT environments. This is coupled with a machine learning system explicitly designed for the automated generation of patterns to identify anomalies, including cybersecurity threats.

The CEP engine's core function is to analyse incoming events in real time. It achieves this by applying a set of predefined patterns written in event process language. The engine generates various complex events, which are subsequently published back to a messaging broker. Furthermore, the CEP engine is responsible for producing the alerts that are presented to the user.

The architecture incorporates an intelligent system. This system is fed by both the simple events and the complex events generated by the CEP engine. Its primary objective is to automatically generate new patterns. These newly generated patterns are then dynamically incorporated into the CEP engine, enabling the continuous monitoring and detection of emerging anomalies.

A notable characteristic of the proposed system is its ability to operate effectively in OT environments where connectivity to extensive data processing infrastructures is constrained. Consequently, an architecture predicated on ARM devices is proposed, leveraging a reduced instruction set computer architecture.

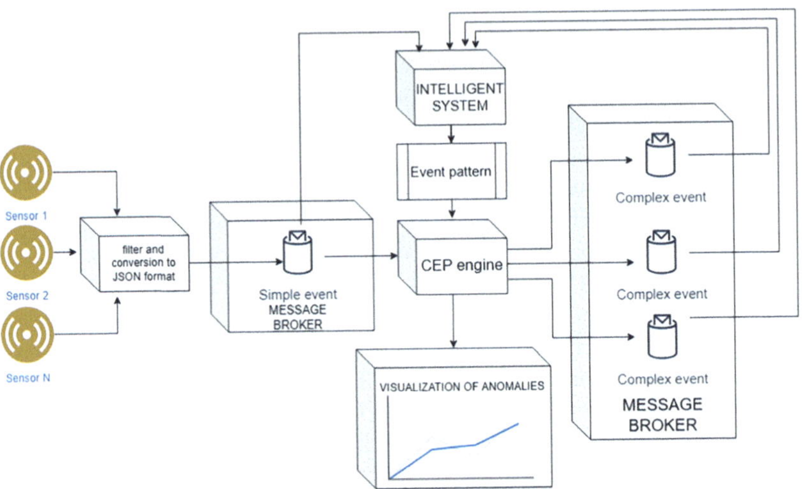

Fig. 1. SEADETEC system architecture [5].

The inherent limitations in computing power and memory within such environments pose significant challenges to the deployment of existing commercial solutions. Furthermore, a key objective of this project is to ensure the sustained performance of MINERVA, the monitored system, without any degradation. For this purpose, the system is deployed on processing boards independent of MINERVA, with the number of boards used being scalable according to processing needs.

The framework's efficacy is validated through its integration into Navantia's MINERVA integrated bridge system within a real-world deployment.

3.2 HMI

In this section, we present the HMI of SEADETEC. The interface is developed in JavaScript using React[1] framework (version 18.3.1). The interface is deployed via Apache in its version 2.4.58, on port 443, in order to be able to use encrypted connections through the use of certificates. Additionally to React, other libraries used for the development of the HMI are:

- Is-ip[2] (version 5.0.1), a simple library for IP address validation. It is used for the generation, by users, of monitoring targets.
- Chart.js[3] (version 4.4.8) for network monitoring visualization. This is a high-performance library and allows the charts to be generated on the client, relieving the server of this task and the computational load it requires. Along with

[1] https://react.dev/.
[2] https://www.npmjs.com/package/is-ip.
[3] https://www.chartjs.org/.

this library, chartjs-adapter-date-fns, version 3.0.0, is used to correctly handle the timestamps shown in the different monitoring graphs.
- Axios[4] (version 1.7.2), which allows all the necessary requests to be made to the API. This library allows to configure the headers in real time, as well as facilitating the handling of the responses and errors received by the API.

The use of React allows an architecture based on highly modular and efficient components, which allows the reuse of these and, in addition, the selective reloading of areas of the page.

The interface contains some configurable files that allow some customization to adapt it to the specific conditions of each environment. The main customization of the interface is the language: it is possible to apply any language to the interface by simply adding the JSON files with the translations and specifying which text file to use in the configuration parameters. Other configuration parameters are: the basic protocols available for the generation of a target, the severity that can be given to the event patterns or the extension of the local data files that store the targets, patterns or monitoring data.

The design of the interface has been designed based on Navantia's MINERVA interface, taking into account compliance with the applicable WCAG 2.1 [15] level A and AA criteria.

All communications, access, or use of the functionalities made from the interface will be encrypted using TLSv1.3. Access and use of the different HMI functionalities and screens offered are controlled by the user's bearer token, which is obtained after login. For each functionality, this token will be required in the API request, and if the user does not have the necessary permissions, they will not have access to the screen or to the required functionalities. Permissions are determined according to the user's role, which can be: operator, expert operator or administrator.

SEADETEC's HMI is designed to align with the logical workflow for detecting cyber anomalies within OT/IoT environments. To achieve this, when deploying the system, the user first has to define the monitoring objective. Following this, they establish the patterns that determine the rules of the CEP engine, which are responsible for activating the alerts. Finally, the user performs a passive monitoring of the system, not only visualising when an alert occurs but also observing a temporal window of their activation, providing crucial context to the events. This entire sequence is explained in further detail in the subsequent sections.

Main Menu Figure 2 shows the screen that is accessed after logging in and serves as the central point from which all other screens can be navigated. It incorporates descriptive text providing information about the framework. In the upper-right corner, the current version of the system is displayed, and in the upper-left corner, the monitoring status is displayed along with the name of the target if available.

[4] https://axios-http.com/.

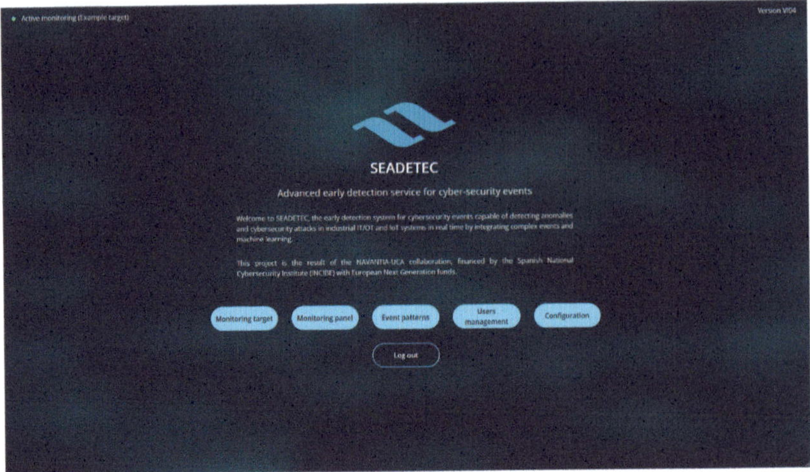

Fig. 2. Main menu screen.

At the bottom of the screen are the buttons through which the main functionalities of the HMI can be reached. The number of buttons that appear may vary according to the user's permissions: an administrator user can access all screens, an expert operator user can access the monitoring target, monitoring panel and event patterns pages, and an operator user can only access the monitoring target and monitoring panel pages.

Pattern Management This screen is used for all tasks related to the administration of the patterns: creation/modification of patterns, generation of new patterns or managing the patterns that are in the CEP engine, such as deploying or deleting them.

Figure 3 illustrates the screen for pattern management, including three sections:

1. The section on the top left hand side where you can enter a new pattern into the system. It is necessary to indicate the pattern name, which must be unique, the pattern itself, and the severity associated with that pattern.
   This section also serves to modify existing patterns. When an existing pattern is being modified, the section title will change to indicate it.
   Finally, two buttons are present: the clear button that clears the name and pattern itself fields, and the save button that saves the new pattern or the modifications made.
2. The section on the bottom left hand side where a table containing all suggested patterns is shown. This includes AI-generated patterns and base patterns, which can be generated by clicking on the buttons found at the top right of the table. Detailed information can be viewed by clicking the eye icon next to each pattern. These patterns can be used to generate a new pattern

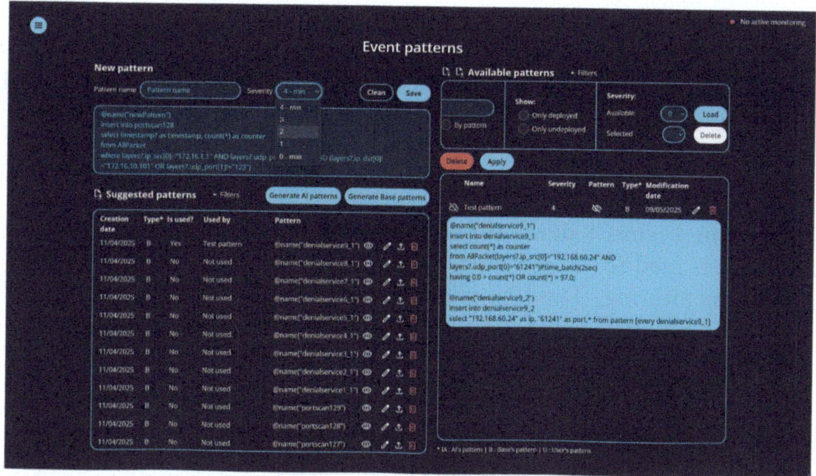

Fig. 3. Pattern management screen.

(pencil symbol) or uploaded without changes (arrow symbol). If uploaded without changes, it will be indicated that they are in use and the name of the pattern from the available patterns table (Available patterns table on the top right hand side) that is using it.

3. The section on the right hand side where the patterns available for use in the CEP engine are shown. Deployed patterns are indicated by a cloud icon, while those not deployed are indicated by a crossed-out cloud icon. To modify or delete these patterns, they must first be undeployed. With these files we can easily transfer the patterns from one system to another.

The patterns shown in both tables are loaded in sets of 50 by 50 to speed up the loading of the screen. The patterns will always be displayed sorted by date of modification or creation, as the case may be, and by their internal ID. It is possible to decide which patterns to display in both tables by using filters, such as the type of pattern, whether they are in use or deployed, the desired date range or the content of the pattern.

Next to both lists of patterns there are two icons in the case of available patterns and one icon in the case of suggested patterns. The common icon in both allows the download of the subset of patterns loaded on the page, while the extra icon found in the available patterns section enables the selection of a local file containing patterns, which are then uploaded to the server for subsequent use. In both cases, since the patterns may contain confidential information, a password is required both to download the file with the patterns and to access the file for uploading. The password must be exactly 32 characters including at least one uppercase letter, one lowercase letter, one number and a “!”, “@”, “#”, “$”, “%”, “^”, “&”, “*”, “(“or”)” symbol.

The patterns will be saved locally in files with extension .seapattern, which will contain in the first line the initialization vector (IV) used to encrypt the set of patterns under the AES-GCM algorithm, and in the following lines the complete set of patterns encrypted with this algorithm using the password indicated by the user.

Target Menu Figure 4 shows the screen for defining a new monitored target.

This page is used to define which network elements are going to be taken into account for monitoring. The IPs, ports, devices and protocols that are selected will be used to filter the network traffic, so that only those network packets that are of interest according to the objective are analysed by the CEP engine.

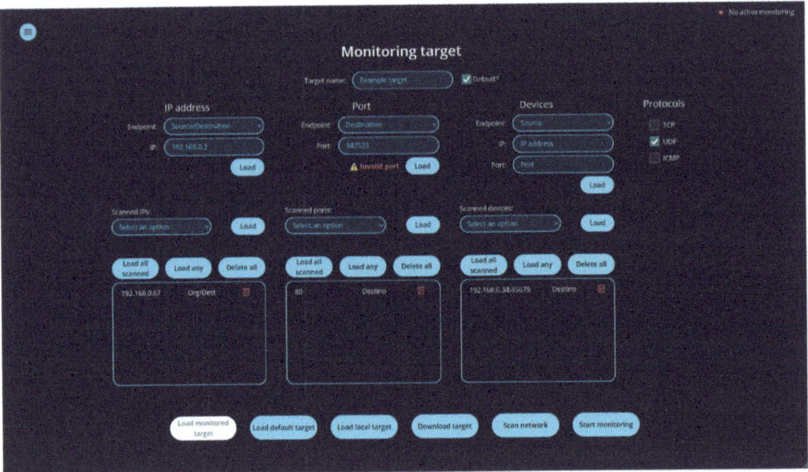

Fig. 4. Target menu screen.

The monitored target can be configured to be the default, such that every time the system is restarted, monitoring of the target is automatically initiated. Whenever the target is designated as the default, it must have a name; otherwise, the name is optional.

The columns for specifying which IPs, ports or devices are to set the target are divided into three sections:

- A first section for manually entering the item to be uploaded. It is necessary to indicate both the value and the endpoint. The value entered will be checked to determine whether it is valid or not. If it is valid, it will be added to the table at the bottom of the column.
- A second section, consisting of a drop-down menu, where all the elements found during a previous scan of the network will be displayed. The duration of this scan can be modified to suit the requirements of the environment. The

scanned items to be loaded can be selected manually or all of them can be loaded using one of the buttons.

- A third section with a table, showing which elements will be taken into account for monitoring, along with three buttons:
  - Load all scanned. To load all scanned elements.
  - Load any. To take into account any IP, port, or device present on the network at the time of monitoring, as it is possible that an item is found that was not present when the scan was performed.
  - Delete all. To remove all loaded elements in the table.

At the bottom of the page, there are a series of buttons offering different functionalities:

- Load monitored target. If active monitoring is present, loads the elements of the monitored target.
- Load default target. If a default target exists, loads the elements of that target.
- Load local target. Allows to select a local .seatarget file to load the target it contains. This type of file contains a specific monitoring target (IPs, ports, devices, protocols, and the name if any) encrypted using AES-GCM, together with the IV that has been used for encryption. Within the file, the IV will be on the first line, followed on subsequent lines by the encrypted target. Encryption of these files shall require a user-entered password which shall have the same conditions as the password used for .seapattern files. With these files, the same targets can be used in different systems without the need to specify them manually.
- Download target. Generates a .seatarget file with the data in the tables, the selected protocols, and the indicated name if any.
- Scan network. Allows a network scan if no active monitoring is present. The elements found on the network are added to the selection options. The scanning time can be configured according to the user's requirements.
- Monitoring panel. Redirects to the monitoring screen. If no monitoring is active, this button allows the initiation of monitoring for the specified target, and the text displayed will be "Start monitoring".

Monitoring Menu Figure 5 shows the monitoring menu when there is an active monitoring. In this screen it is possible to visualise, in real time, the alerts generated by the patterns deployed in the CEP engine. The alerts will be displayed on two screens: the main one when entering the page, where you can see four graphs showing the current status of the alerts that have occurred, and a drop-down menu where you can see a history of the alerts, both active and resolved, along with detailed information on each one of them.

The four charts displayed on the main screen will be:

- Top left: Time window with the instants (X-axis) where an alert generated by a pattern is triggered (Y-axis). It will be indicated with a 1 in the instant that

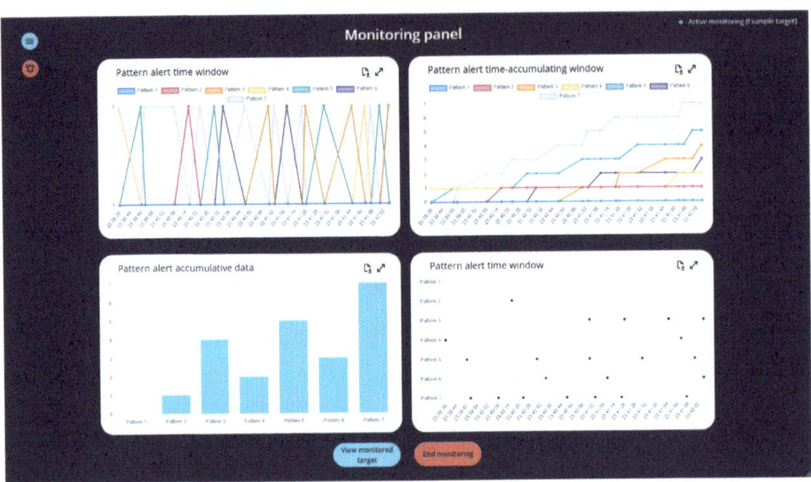

Fig. 5. Monitoring menu screen.

the alert has been activated and with a 0 in the instant that it has not been activated. Each line of the graph represents each of the patterns deployed in the CEP engine used for monitoring.

- Top right: Time window with the number of accumulated alerts (Y-axis) generated by a deployed pattern for each time instant (X-axis) where an alert has been activated. The cumulative is reset to 0 at the start of a monitoring.
- Bottom left: Accumulated alerts generated (X-axis) for each pattern deployed (Y-axis) in the CEP engine. The accumulated counts since the beginning of the monitoring.
- Right left: Time window with the instants (X-axis) where an alert generated by a deployed pattern (Y-axis) is activated. Each point on the graph represents the time when an alert has been triggered.

There are two buttons below the graphs:

- Monitored target: if there is an active monitoring, view the monitored target data. If there is no monitoring, the button is used to go to the target menu screen and the displayed text will be "Monitoring target".
- End monitoring: ends of current monitoring. If no monitoring is active, the last monitoring or the default monitoring will be activated if no monitoring has been started previously. The displayed text will be "Resume monitoring".

In the case of accessing this screen without any active monitoring, the message "No active monitoring" will be displayed instead of the four panels.

Access to the alerts menu is through the button under the side menu button. If there is at least one active alert, the button will be displayed in red with a vibrating bell icon, while if there is no active alert the button will be displayed in the same blue as the side menu button and with a static bell icon.

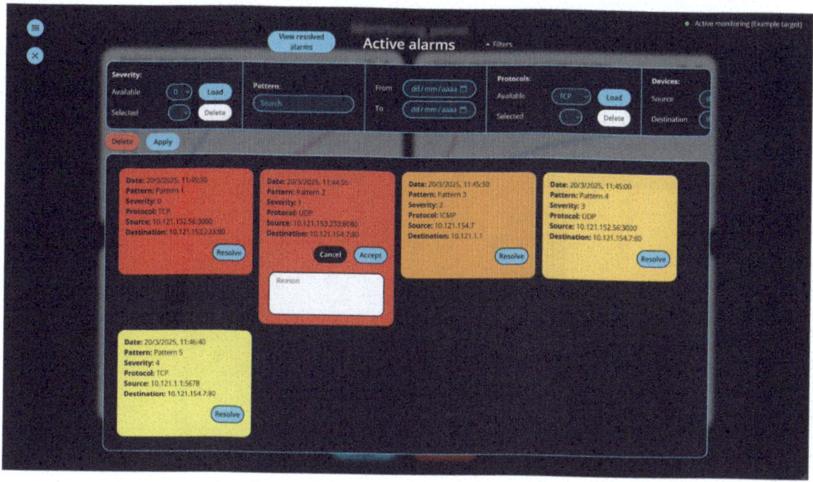

Fig. 6. Alert menu screen.

Alert Menu Figure 6 shows active alerts up to the current time, regardless of whether they belong to the current monitoring session or not, in order from most to least severe and from most recent to least. Each alert is colour-coded according to the severity associated with the pattern that generates it, ranging from the most intense red when the severity is maximum to yellow when the severity is minimum. Along with the severity information, more information about the alert is displayed, such as the source and destination devices, the pattern that generates the alert or the instant at which it is triggered. Filters can be applied to this information to obtain only the necessary alerts, similar to how they are applied to patterns.

Each of the alerts can be resolved by indicating, optionally, the reason for the resolution. The user who has indicated the alert as resolved will also be automatically stored.

To view the resolved alerts, click on the button next to the title. This button is used to switch between active and resolved alerts.

Resolved Alerts Menu Figure 7 displays the alerts that have been marked as resolved, along with the reason given and the user who resolved them. All resolved alerts will be coloured green regardless of the severity associated with them.

These alerts will be displayed sorted by severity and by date, and filters can be applied to them to select a subset of them, as with active alerts.

Each of the alerts can be reactivated, returning to the previous screen. In the case of reactivation, the information corresponding to the reason for the resolution and the user who has indicated it as resolved will be deleted or overwritten in the case of a new resolution.

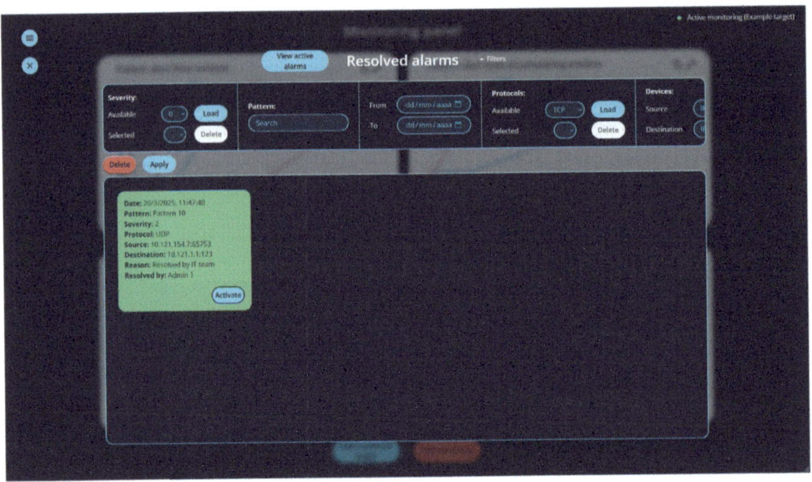

Fig. 7. Resolved alerts menu screen.

4 Conclusions and Future Work

This paper successfully presents the implementation of a cybersecurity framework that leverages complex event processing and a human-machine interface. This framework is specifically tailored for operational technology and Internet of Things environments and has been validated within Navantia's MINERVA integrated bridge system. The research directly addresses the growing cybersecurity vulnerabilities present in the hyper-connected systems of Industry 4.0, where traditional IT-centric security solutions often prove inadequate.

Key achievements of this work include the effective implementation of a framework capable of capturing network traffic and utilizing a CEP engine for automated anomaly detection. Furthermore, the real-world validation of this framework within Navantia's MINERVA system demonstrates its practical applicability and efficacy in a demanding industrial context. The architecture's resource-conscious design, based on ARM devices, acknowledges the limitations of OT/IoT environments. The developed HMI offers a user-friendly interface for managing monitoring targets, event patterns, and alerts, accommodating different user roles. The design of the HMI prioritizes practical needs by aligning with the existing MINERVA interface and adhering to accessibility standards. Finally, the framework incorporates enhanced security measures, such as encrypted communication and role-based access control, ensuring system integrity and confidentiality. In essence, this research represents a step forward towards real-time, adaptable cybersecurity frameworks tailored to OT/IoT constraints for the increasingly interconnected industrial landscape of Industry 4.0.

Building upon the successful implementation and validation of this framework, several promising avenues for future research and development emerge:

- Integration of machine learning for dynamic pattern generation: While the current framework utilizes CEP for real-time detection, future work could focus on a tighter integration with the previously proposed machine learning system. This could enable the automated and dynamic generation of new anomaly detection patterns, enhancing the system's ability to identify novel and evolving threats without constant manual updates.
- Enhanced anomaly analysis and forensics: Future research could explore incorporating more sophisticated analytical capabilities within the framework. This might include advanced visualization techniques for detected anomalies, root cause analysis tools, and forensic features to better understand the nature and impact of cyber incidents.
- Predictive cybersecurity: Investigating the potential of using the collected and processed data to develop predictive models could be a valuable future direction. This could involve leveraging machine learning to forecast potential future attacks based on observed trends and patterns.
- Expansion to other industrial sectors: The demonstrated success within the maritime navigation system suggests the potential for adapting and deploying this framework in other Industry 4.0 sectors with similar cybersecurity challenges, such as manufacturing, energy, and transportation.
- Improved scalability and distributed deployment: Future work could address the scalability of the framework for larger and more complex industrial deployments. Exploring distributed CEP engines and data processing techniques could enhance the system's ability to handle vast amounts of data from numerous interconnected devices.
- Advanced HMI features: Further development of the HMI could include features like customizable dashboards, more detailed alert information and reporting, integration with other security tools, and enhanced user management capabilities.
- Evaluation against a broader range of cyberattacks: While the paper mentions real-world deployment, future work could involve rigorous testing and evaluation of the framework against a wider spectrum of known and simulated cyberattacks to further validate its robustness and effectiveness.
- Exploration of explainable AI for anomaly detection: If machine learning is further integrated, research into explainable AI techniques could provide insights into why certain patterns are flagged as anomalies, increasing user trust and facilitating better incident response.

These potential future directions highlight the ongoing nature of cybersecurity research and the continuous need for innovation to address the evolving threat landscape within Industry 4.0. The foundation laid by this work provides a strong platform for these advancements.

Acknowledgements. The CPP001/22_NAVANTIA-SEADETEC project publication is the result of work co-funded by National Institute of Cybersecurity and the European Union's Recovery and Resilience Facility through the Recovery, Transformation and Resilience Plan. The authors' views do not necessarily represent those of the funding entities. This publication is also part of the I+D+i grant PID2021-122215NB-C33 funded by MICIU/AEI/10.13039/501100011033 and by ERDF/EU, and by the Spanish Ministry of Science and Innovation under the Excellence Network AI4Software (Red2022-134647-T).

References

1. Buczak, A.L., Guven, E.: A survey of data mining and machine learning methods for cyber security intrusion detection. IEEE Commun. Surv. Tutor. **18**(2), 1153–1176 (2016). https://doi.org/10.1109/COMST.2015.2494502
2. Crowdstrike: Global threat report (2021). https://www.crowdstrike.com/en-us/resources/reports/global-threat-report-2021/. Accessed 05 June 2025
3. Dasgupta, D., Akhtar, Z., Sen, S.: Machine learning in cybersecurity: a comprehensive survey. J. Def. Model. Simul. **19**(1) (2022). https://doi.org/10.1177/1548512920951275
4. Dhirani, L.L., Armstrong, E., Newe, T.: Industrial IoT, cyber threats, and standards landscape: evaluation and roadmap. Sensors **21**(11) (2021). https://doi.org/10.3390/s21113901
5. Domínguez-Jiménez, J.J., Gómez Sánchez, R., Medina-Bulo, I., Boubeta-Puig, J., Rodríguez-García, M., Muñoz-Ortega, A., Balderas-Díaz, S., Guerrero-Contreras, G., Silva-Ramírez, E., Luna-Ramos, P., Carretero Henares, J., Molina Cabrera, A., Fuentes Landi, G., Torres Gómez., P.: SEADETEC: Advanced service for early detection of cybersecurity events. In: International Conference on Industry Sciences and Computer Sciences Innovation (2024). https://iscsi-conference.org/. Accessed 06 June 2025
6. Gharibian, F., Ghorbani, A.A.: Comparative study of supervised machine learning techniques for intrusion detection. In: Fifth Annual Conference on Communication Networks and Services Research (CNSR '07), pp. 350–358 (2007). https://doi.org/10.1109/CNSR.2007.22
7. INCIBE: Compra pública de innovación. https://www.incibe.es/industria-cpi. Accessed 07 May 2025
8. Markets and Markets: Industry 4.0 market by technology (industrial robots, blockchain, industrial sensors, industrial 3D printing, machine vision, HMI, AI in manufacturing, digital twin, AGV's, machine condition monitoring) and geography—global forecast to 2026 (2021). https://www.researchandmarkets.com/reports/5353576/industry-4-0-market-by-technology-industrial. Accessed 05 June 2025
9. Meidan, Y., Bohadana, M., Shabtai, A., Guarnizo, J.D., Ochoa, M., Tippenhauer, N.O., Elovici, Y.: ProfilIoT: a machine learning approach for IoT device identification based on network traffic analysis. In: Proceedings of the Symposium on Applied Computing, pp. 506–509. SAC '17, Association for Computing Machinery, New York, NY, USA (2017). https://doi.org/10.1145/3019612.3019878
10. Roldán-Gómez, J., Martínez del Rincon, J., Boubeta-Puig, J., Martínez, J.L.: An automatic unsupervised complex event processing rules generation architecture for real-time IoT attacks detection. Wirel. Netw. **30**(6) (2024). https://doi.org/10.1007/s11276-022-03219-y
11. Roldán, J., Boubeta-Puig, J., Martínez, J.L., Ortiz, G.: Integrating complex event processing and machine learning: an intelligent architecture for detecting IoT security attacks. Expert. Syst. Appl. **149** (2020). https://doi.org/10.1016/j.eswa.2020.113251

12. Sauter, T., Treytl, A.: IoT-enabled sensors in automation systems and their security challenges. IEEE Sens. Lett. **7**(12) (2023). https://doi.org/10.1109/LSENS.2023.3332404
13. Süzen, A.A.: A risk-assessment of cyber attacks and defense strategies in industry 4.0 ecosystem. Int. J. Comput. Netw. Inf. Secur. **12**(1) (2020). https://doi.org/10.5815/ijcnis.2020.01.01
14. Symantec: Internet security threat report (2019). https://docs.broadcom.com/doc/istr-24-2019-en. Accessed 05 June 2025
15. W3C: Web Content Accessibility Guidelines (WCAG) 2.1 (2018). https://www.w3.org/TR/WCAG21/. Accessed 14 May 2025

Influence of Timestamp in a Complex System for the Detection of Cyberattacks

Leopoldo Gutiérrez-Galeano(✉), Francisco Palomo-Lozano, Juan-José Domínguez-Jiménez, and Inmaculada Medina-Bulo

Escuela Superior de Ingeniería, University of Cadiz, Puerto Real, Spain
leopoldo.gutierrez@uca.es, francisco.palomo@uca.es, juanjose.dominguez@uca.es, inmaculada.medina@uca.es

Abstract. Cybersecurity is constantly evolving due to emerging cyberthreats. Traditional security measures could help mitigate known threats, but they are not effective against new types of attacks. Therefore, it is necessary to explore innovative and effective mitigation strategies to deal with any type of attack, known or emerging. Traditional cybersecurity techniques based on Artificial Intelligence (AI) often rely on Artificial Neural Networks (ANN) designed from scratch. This paper introduces a novel approach based on a complex system that fine-tunes a pre-trained ANN-based Natural Language Processing (NLP) model, which is thus transformed for cyberattack detection. The resulting model can classify network traffic as benign or malicious. This anomaly-based classifier analyzes the statistics of network flows by identifying deviations that are indicative of potential attacks. This paper presents the results of a series of experiments, specifically designed to evaluate the performance by using different sizes of the base model, as well as the influence of the timestamp. The source NLP model used is T5 with the sizes "t5-small" and "t5-base", while the dataset selected is CIC-IDS-2017. Rigorous evaluation using Stratified 5-Fold Cross-Validation proves the effectiveness of our approach, achieving up to 99.96% of accuracy, precision, recall and F-score, all of them as weighted metrics. These promising results underscore the potential of this novel technique in improving cybersecurity defenses.

Keywords: Cybersecurity · Deep Learning · Fine Tuning · Natural Language Processing · CIC-IDS-2017

1 Introduction

Cybersecurity has become an increasingly critical concern due to the continuous emergence of new and sophisticated cyberthreats. The diverse range of potential attacks on computer systems requires a custom approach that combines various techniques and tools to minimize their impact. However, the ever-evolving landscape of cybercrime, where attackers constantly develop novel techniques,

J. Schäfer and J. Boubeta-Puig (Eds.): SGSOACS 2025, CCIS 2831, pp. 132–147, 2026.
https://doi.org/10.1007/978-3-032-14816-2_11

presents a significant challenge. Consequently, safeguarding sensitive information, a vital organizational asset, remains a paramount objective.

The continuous emergence of new attack techniques requires the development of cyberattack detection systems capable of identifying novel threats. AI, particularly Deep Learning (DL), offers a promising way to achieve this goal. DL models, composed of multiple layers of interconnected neurons, are capable of learning complex patterns from a vast amount of data. This powerful technique has revolutionized fields such as NLP, image recognition, and speech recognition. By applying DL to analyze network flow statistics, we can build robust AI systems capable of detecting cyberattacks.

The design and evaluation of a complex DL-based cyberattacks detection system requires a sufficiently large and varied dataset. The selected dataset, CIC-IDS-2017 [19], contains captures of network traces where both benign and malicious packets circulate, identifying various types of attacks. CIC-IDS-2017 is characterized by having a set of properties that allow identifying when there is or is not a cyberattack. Our objective is to carry out a study of the influence of each property on the results of a cyberattacks detection system.

We designed and evaluated a cyberattacks detection system based on a DL model, by fine-tuning a pre-trained NLP model. More concretely, we decided to select the T5 [10] model, using the SimpleT5 wrapper [11]. SimpleT5 is a wrapper built over PyTorch, to perform fine-tuning of T5 without modifying its architecture. Various snapshots of this model, each with different sizes, are available to be directly deployed for NLP tasks or to be fine-tuned. For our approach, we chose the fine-tuning technique with t5-small and t5-base models, since we were interested in keeping the whole model architecture, obtaining our model by updating all the weights of T5.

One of the most interesting features is the timestamp. This feature was selected due to its potential temporal influence on the model, since the date and time embedded within it could introduce biases or patterns affecting the resulting model. Therefore, we started studying the mentioned feature, together with the size of the selected base models, applying our methodology to the selected dataset.

The current paper is structured as follows: Sect. 2 contains papers related to the strategy used in the current paper, as well as using any other strategy based on Machine Learning; Sect. 3 describes the data we used for our experiments, in addition to its source; In Sect. 4 the environment we set up for the performed experiments is described, as well as the description of the designed experiments; Sect. 5 shows the results after carrying out the designed experiments, including an analysis of results of all the experiments together; Sect. 6 contains the conclusions and future work.

2 State of the Art

2.1 Datasets

The availability of robust public datasets for the task we are carrying out is very limited. The following are some of the most relevant datasets in this domain:

- **KDD Cup 1999** [22]: Published by University of California (UC), Irvine in 1999, it's an updated version of DARPA98 and has been widely used for academic IDS research.
- **NSL-KDD** [17]: Released in 2009 as an improved version of KDD Cup 1999, addressing several issues found in the original dataset.
- **UNSW-NB15** [23]: Created by the University of New South Wales (UNSW) for research, it includes 9 attack types and 49 features from network traffic captured over two time periods.
- **CIC-IDS-2017** [13,19]: Published by the Canadian Institute for Cybersecurity (CIC) due to limitations in older datasets, it contains benign traffic and 14 attack types with 84 network flow features, generated with their CICFlowMeter [18] tool.
- **CSE-CIC-IDS2018** [13,21]: A collaboration between CIC and the Communications Security Establishment (CSE), it mirrors the structure of CIC-IDS-2017 but was generated in an AWS environment and remains a modern dataset for IDS research. It was also generated using CICFlowMeter.
- **CIC-DDoS2019** [14,20]: Another dataset from CIC, specifically focused on a taxonomy of Distributed Denial of Service (DDoS) attacks. The CICFlowMeter tool was also used to generate this dataset.
- **AWID2** [2] **and AWID3** [4]: Published by the University of the Aegean, these datasets are based on 802.11 networks, with AWID2 focusing on attack signatures and AWID3 including more recent and multi-layered attacks.
- **BCCC-CIC-IDS-2017** [3,12]: An augmented version of CIC-IDS-2017, released in 2025 by the Behaviour-Centric Cybersecurity Center (BCCC), it contains 122 features generated with their NTLFlowLyzer tool.

Table 1 contains information about all the aforementioned datasets. We have selected the CIC-IDS-2017 dataset for this research since it is still widely used, it contains a wide variety of the most popular and up-to-date types of attacks, and it contains quite a lot of records to build a promising model.

2.2 Techniques

In order to gain a comprehensive understanding of the research landscape in DL-based cyberattacks detection models, we analyzed several relevant papers.

- **Abdel-Basset et al.** [1] proposed SS-Deep-ID, evaluating it on CIC-IDS-2017. Notable results: 99.69% accuracy, 92.31% precision, 96.29% recall, 94.18% F-score. Authors highlighted superior performance over other works for metrics.

Table 1. Datasets for detection of cyberattacks

Dataset	Published by	Year	Attack types	Features	Records
KDD Cup 1999	UC	1999	4	41	4,898,431
NSL-KDD	CIC	2009	22	41	125,973
UNSW-NB15	UNSW	2015	9	49	2,540,047
CIC-IDS-2017	CIC	2017	14	84	2,830,743
CSE-CIC-IDS2018	CIC and CSE	2018	14	84	16,232,943
CIC-DDoS2019	CIC	2019	18	84	12,794,627
AWID2	UA	2016	3	155	42,388,298
AWID3	UA	2021	13	253	15,574,911
BCCC-CIC-IDS-2017	BCCC	2025	13	122	2,438,052

- **Wang et al.** [24] introduced a GA-BPNN model for network security. Applied to CIC-IDS-2017, yielding 98% accuracy, 98.5% precision, 95% recall, and 96.5% F-score.
- **Maruthupandi et al.** [9] presented IADCL, applied to CIC-IDS-2017. Achieved 99.70% accuracy, 99.72% precision, 99.70% recall, 99.71% F-score. Compared with Immune Net, XGBoost, RF, DT, LR.
- **Guo et al.** [5] proposed TRBMA (BS-OSS) with Borderline SMOTE-OSS. Evaluated on CIC-IDS-2017, obtaining high results: 99.88% accuracy, 99.86% precision, 99.88% recall, 99.89% F-score.
- **Hariharan et al.** [7] introduced a Hybrid Deep Learning Model for NIDS using Seq2Seq and ConvLSTM. Applied to CIC-IDS-2017, reporting 99% accuracy, 97% precision, 96% recall, 97% F-score.
- **Tapu et al.** [16] proposed a novel hybrid meta-deep learning approach for detecting packet data. Utilized Siamese and Prototypical networks on CIC-IDS-2017. Achieved 95.68% accuracy, 96.50% precision, 95.68% recall, 96.10% F-score.
- **Li et al.** [8] proposed HDFEF for IDS and presented results for CIC-IDS-2017. Specific results: 99.73% precision, 99.96% recall, 99.84% F-score. Accuracy not provided in the text.
- **Yilmaz et al.** [25] investigated RF, CatBoost, LightGBM, XGBoost for NIDS on CIC-IDS-2017. Using RF: 93% precision, 71% recall, 74% F-score. Accuracy not reported for these algorithms.

3 Data Structure

The data we are using as input consist of statistics of network flows. They are included in several CSV files provided in the selected dataset. These files were generated by the CICFlowMeter tool, taking PCAP files as input.

PCAP files contain records of captured network packets. We could find relevant information such as the source IP address, destination IP address, port, timestamp, protocol, payload, and so on. Some of this data is also found in the CSV files. Hence, we could obtain the CSV files in two different ways: we could use the already generated CSV files, as an offline dataset for research purposes; or, in a real system, we could capture network traffic packets to obtain statistics of network flows by the use of CICFlowMeter as an Extract, Transform, and Load (ETL) tool, using real data, in a real environment, in real time.

In the dataset we found rows of data regarding benign packets and 14 different types of attacks. Table 2 presents all these categories, along with the numerical labels assigned in our system and the corresponding number of packets for each type. These counts reflect the dataset's composition after a standard cleaning process, which involved removing duplicate rows and columns with constant values.

Table 2. Types of attacks found in CIC-IDS-2017 and assigned labels

Type of attack (original label)	New label	Count
BENIGN	0	419043
DoS hulk	1	172846
PortScan	2	90694
DDoS	3	128014
DoS goldenEye	4	10286
FTP-Patator	5	5931
SSH-Patator	6	3219
DoS slowloris	7	5385
DoS slowhttptest	8	5228
Bot	9	1948
Web attack - Brute force	10	1470
Web attack - XSS	11	652
Infiltration	12	36
Web attack - Sql injection	13	21
Heartbleed	14	11

3.1 Input Representation for T5 Model

A main aspect of adapting the T5 model, primarily designed as an encoder-decoder architecture for text-to-text tasks, to tabular network flow data lies in effectively representing numerical features as sequential input compatible with its tokenizer. In this work, we adopted the input representation strategy previously established and detailed in our prior research [6].

Specifically, for each network flow (row) in the CIC-IDS-2017 dataset, all numerical features were first converted into string representations and then sequentially concatenated using the character | as a delimiter. This concatenation resulted in a single continuous string for each network flow, which served as the direct input to the pre-trained T5 tokenizer.

The detailed architecture of our fine-tuning system for cyberattack detection, including the comprehensive hyperparameter tuning process for the fine-tuning stage, was presented in our prior work [6]. This research established the optimal hyperparameter settings employed in the current study.

4 Experiments Configuration

Before performing the main experiments, we configured the necessary software and hardware resources. In this section, relevant information regarding the experiments environment as well as the experiments design can be found.

4.1 Experiments Environment

As mentioned previously, we selected the T5 model for our experiments using the SimpleT5 wrapper. More concretely, we made use of the two smallest sizes, *t5-small* and *t5-base*. SimpleT5 has several hyperparameters available for use, which we carefully analysed to select the most appropriate values for some and identify others to be optimised. In particular, we use the following hyperparameters: *max_epochs* with value 10, *target_max_token_len* with value 3, *batch_size* with value 16, *precision* with value 32, and *source_max_token_len* with value 150. We chose a public dataset for our experiments, which is CIC-IDS-2017. This dataset contains the latest and most common types of cyberattacks.

We carried out the main experiments on a powerful supercomputer at the University of Cádiz. This supercomputer has several nodes with 2 CPUs with 64 cores and 256 GB of RAM each, 4 of them with NVIDIA A100 GPU cards with 40 GB of memory each. Moreover, it contains 2 nodes with more memory, 1 TB per node instead of 256 GB.

4.2 Experiments Design

In order to ensure a robust model evaluation, we decided to apply the Stratified 5-Fold Cross-Validation technique for all the experiments included in our design. We split the dataset into two main parts: 80% for training and validation, and 20% for testing. Using the mentioned technique, we divided the training and validation data into five folds. For each fold, one part was used for validation (16%), while the remaining four parts were used for training (64%). This process was repeated five times, allowing for a comprehensive assessment of the model's performance.

The models perform a classification task. Basically, given an input based on statistics of network flows, each model is able to predict if it is benign or malicious, which in the second case, the model directly outputs the type of attack.

The experiments detailed in this section have been designed with the purpose of testing different variations based on a slight variation of features in the selected dataset and different snapshots of the pre-trained model. The selected dataset is CIC-IDS-2017. Previously, we performed a data cleaning task which included the homogenisation of column names, the removal of useless columns, columns with unique values and columns with high correlation, and the removal of duplicated rows and those with empty and null values. After cleaning, we were interested in studying the influence of timestamp on the model. Therefore, the slight variation of features is the use of all the features and the use of all of them except timestamp. We selected this feature because we would like to study if it could influence the model, due to its potential temporal, since the date and time embedded within it could introduce biases or patterns affecting the resulting model. Finally, the last variation is related to the snapshots of the selected model, T5, which are the use of the smallest sizes of this model: t5-small and t5-base.

Therefore, given the aforementioned variations, we designed four distintc experiments to evaluate the influence of the T5 model size and the inclusion of the timestamp feature on cyberattack detection using the CIC-IDS-2017 dataset. Each experiment involved fine-tuning a T5 model on the cleaned dataset. Experiments 1 and 2 utilized the t5-small model, with Experiment 1 including all features (timestamp included) and Experiment 2 excluding the timestamp. Similarly, Experiments 3 and 4 employed the t5-base model; Experiment 3 incorporated all features (timestamp included), while Experiment 4 omitted the timestamp. This systematic design allowed for a direct assessment of each factor's impact on model performance.

5 Experiments Results

For each experiment we performed a *Fine-Tuning* task using the *Stratified 5-Fold CV* approach, which executes 5 different *Fine-Tuning* processes, each one of them with its related pair of training and validation subsets. For each fold, since we configured the execution of 10 epochs, we obtained 10 model snapshots. Therefore, for each fold, we obtained the predictions using the validation subsets in order to select the best epoch, and finally, for the best one, we obtained the predictions using the test subset, which the model has never seen. We used these test predictions to calculate the values for each one of the selected metrics, for each fold, and to finish the whole process, we calculated the *mean* and the *standard deviation*, for each metric.

To be able to compare our results, we used the following weighted metrics [15]: *accuracy*, *precision*, *recall* and *F-score*. The selected metrics are the most suitable for classification models. Afterwards, we describe in detail the results we obtained. Therefore, in the following subsections, one for each experiment, the results for the aforementioned metrics, a confusion matrix, and an analysis of results can be found.

5.1 Analysis of Results

To facilitate a comprehensive analysis and comparison of our experiments, as well as to enable benchmarking against related publications in Sect. 2.2, we utilized a set of established performance metrics. Specifically, we employed accuracy, precision, recall, F1-score, and false positive rate. These metrics were selected because they offer a comprehensive evaluation of our system's ability to accurately detect cyberattacks while minimizing false alarms, which are critical considerations in real-world deployment.

In general, we could classify our experiments into different groups: using all the features (odd experiments) or all of them without timestamp (even experiments), either using the smallest size of T5, t5-small (the first pair of experiments, 1–2), or the second smallest size, t5-base (the last pair of experiments, 3–4).

In Table 3 all the results for all the experiments performed can be found. Looking at the table mentioned, we can affirm the following facts:

- The best overall performance was achieved in experiment 3, utilizing the t5-base model with all features, including timestamp, yielding a remarkable 99,96% across al metrics. Only 1 out of 2500 flows are unsuccessfully classified.
- Our results consistently show that including the timestamp feature leads to slightly better performance in both t5-small and t5-base configurations. While all experiments yielded high accuracy, the timestamp-inclusive models consistently outperformed their counterparts by approximately 0,02–0,27% in accuracy (comparing experiments 1 vs. 2, and experiments 3 vs. 4). This suggests that temporal information, even when processed by a model originally designed for text, aids in capturing nuanced patterns in network flow statistics. The timestamp likely enables the T5 model to infer the sequential context and temporal dynamics of network events, such as event frequency, duration of flows, or the order of suspicious activities. These temporal correlations can be crucial in distinguishing sophisticated attack patterns from benign traffic, as many cyberattacks unfold over specific timeframes or in particular sequences.
- For both feature sets (with and without timestamp), using the larger t5-base model consistently resulted in slightly better performance compared to t5-small. This indicates that the increased parameter count of t5-base allows for a richer representation of the input data, leading to marginally improved detection capabilities.
- All evaluated metrics remained consistently high and stable across all experiments, reinforcing the robutsness of our approach and ensuring a balanced assessment of the effectivenes of our model.

Overall, the fine-tuning of pre-trained T5 models demonstrates significant promise for real-time cyberattack detection, with the t5-base model leveraging timestamp information proving to be the most effective configuration.

Table 3. Experiments results

Experiment	Model size	Included timestamp	Accuracy	Precision	Recall	F-score
1	t5-small	Yes	99.94	99.94	99.94	99.94
2	t5-small	No	99.69	99.73	99.69	99.69
3	t5-base	Yes	**99.96**	**99.96**	**99.96**	**99.96**
4	t5-base	No	99.78	99.77	99.78	99.75

Values expressed as percentages (%)

5.2 Detailed Confusion Matrices

For a more granular understanding of our model's classification performance across all classes and for each experiment, detailed confusion matrices are provided in Fig. 1. The confusion matrices for each of the four experiments offer a comprehensive, class-by-class visualisation of our models' predictive performance. Each matrix distinctly illustrates the counts of correctly classified instances (true positives and true negatives) and misclassified instances (false positives and false negatives) across all 15 classes (comprising benign traffic and 14 distinct attack types).

A consistency in performance is discernible across all experiments, particularly evident for the highly prevalent 'Benign' class and a significant number of the common attack types (e.g., DDoS, PortScan). The diagonal elements of these matrices, representing true positives, are consistently robust for these dominant classes, underscoring the models' strong capability to accurately identify the vast majority of network traffic. This performance directly underpins the exceptionally high overall accuracy, precision, recall, and F-score values reported in Table 3.

A inspection of the individual matrices reveals important differences attributable to the experimental configurations. Consistent with our analysis (Sect. 5.1), models trained with the timestamp feature (experiments 1 and 3, Fig. 1a and c, respectively) generally exhibit cleaner confusion matrices. This is particularly evident in the subtly reduced number of misclassifications for certain attack types. This observation corroborates our hypothesis that the provision of temporal context significantly assists the T5 model in discerning more complex attack patterns, presumably by enabling it to learn the sequential nature or temporal duration inherent in malicious activities.

Also, the t5-base models (experiments 3 and 4, Fig. 1c and d respectively) consistently demonstrate marginally superior performance across various classes compared to their t5-small counterparts. This incremental improvement is often manifested by slightly higher true positive counts and marginally lower false positive/negative counts for a broader spectrum of attack types, suggesting that the larger model benefits from an increased capacity to capture and represent intricate features within the network flow data.

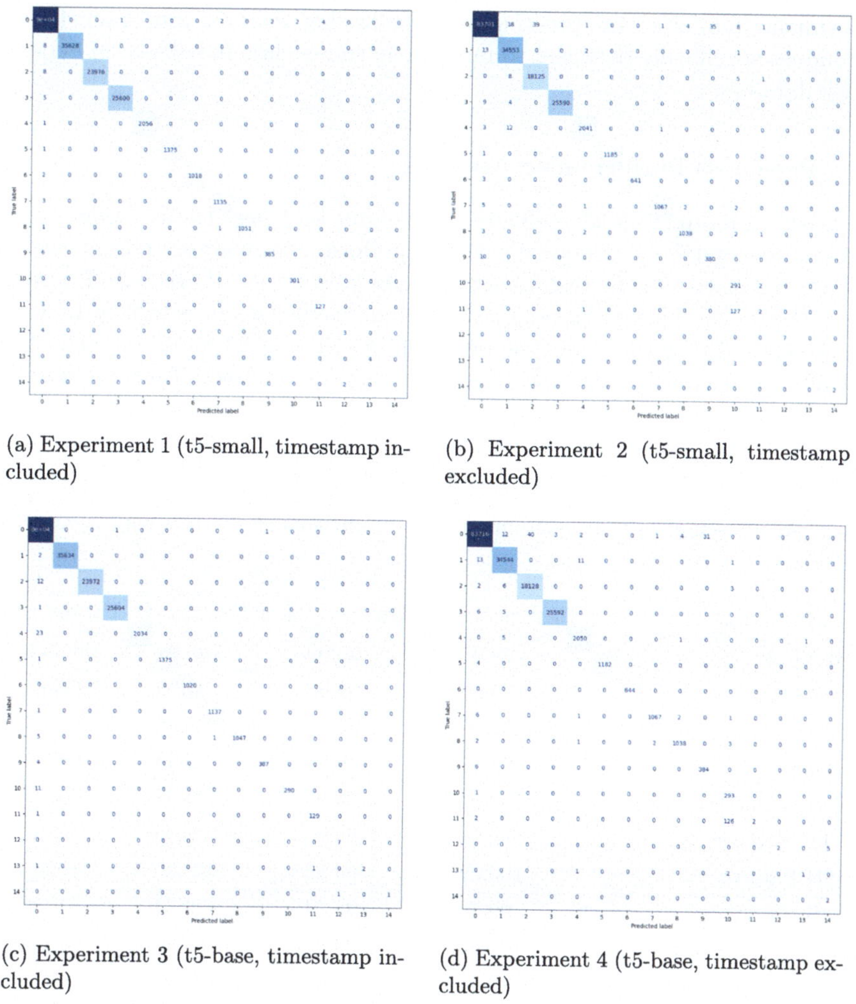

(a) Experiment 1 (t5-small, timestamp included)

(b) Experiment 2 (t5-small, timestamp excluded)

(c) Experiment 3 (t5-base, timestamp included)

(d) Experiment 4 (t5-base, timestamp excluded)

Fig. 1. Confusion matrices for all four experiments.

The confusion matrices underscore the pervasive impact of class imbalance on model performance. While major attack categories are robustly detected, certain minority classes, notably SQL Injection (label 13) and Infiltration (label 12), exhibit comparatively lower numbers of true positives. Furthermore, these rare classes show a discernible tendency to be misclassified as other attack types or, at times, even as benign traffic. For instance, considering experiment 4 (Fig. 1d), the confusion matrix for Web Attack XSS (level 11) might reveal a noticeable proportion of instances incorrectly classified as Web Attack - Brute force (label 10), indicating the model's inherent difficulty in learning distinct patterns for these significantly under-represented categories. This observation across the experiments reinforces the pressing need for further research into sophisticated techniques specifically designed to mitigate extreme class imbalance in cybersecurity datasets.

5.3 Per-Class Performance Analysis

To provide a more granular understanding of our best-performing model's effectiveness, we conducted a detailed per-class performance analysis. This is particularly crucial given the inherent class imbalance within the CIC-IDS-2017 dataset, where the overall high accuracy might obscure challenges in detecting minority attack types. Table 4 presents the precision, recall, and F1-score for each of the 15 traffic classes, alongside their respective support (number of instances in the test set), for experiment 1. The other experiments present similar values, so the analysis is similar.

Table 4. Per-class performance metrics for experiment 1 (t5-small, timestamp included)

Class label	Precision (%)	Recall (%)	F1-score (%)	Support
BENIGN	99.95	99.99	99.97	89944
DoS hulk	100.00	99.98	99.99	35636
PortScan	100.00	99.97	99.98	23984
DDoS	99.99	99.98	99.99	25605
DoS goldenEye	100.00	99.95	99.98	2057
FTP-Patator	100.00	99.93	99.96	1376
SSH-Patator	100.00	99.80	99.90	1020
DoS slowloris	99.74	99.74	99.74	1138
DoS slowhttptest	100.00	99.81	99.90	1053
Bot	99.48	98.47	98.97	391
Web attack - Brute Force	99.34	100.00	99.67	301
Web attack - XSS	96.95	97.69	97.32	130
Infiltration	60.00	42.86	50.00	7
Web attack - Sql injection	100.00	100.00	100.00	4
Heartbleed	**0.00**	**0.00**	**0.00**	**2**

The analysis in Table 4 reveals several critical insights into the model's performance on imbalanced classes. For the majority of attack types and benign traffic, our model achieves exceptionally high performance, with precision, recall, and F1-scores consistently approaching 100%. This is evident in classes such as BENIGN, DoS Hulk, PortScan, and DDoS, which also represent the largest proportions of the dataset.

However, the table distinctly highlights the challenges associated with detecting very rare attack types. Specifically, Infiltration and Heartbleed exhibit significantly lower performance. For Infiltration, with only 7 instances in the test set, the model achieves a precision of 60.00% and a recall of 42.86%, leading to an F1-score of 50.00%. This indicates that while the model identifies some instances correctly, it also generates a notable number of false positives or fails to detect a substantial portion of actual attacks.

The most challenging case is Heartbleed, for which the model reports 0.00% on all metrics. With only 2 instances in the test set, this class is extremely under-represented, making it exceedingly difficult for the model to learn any meaningful patterns. The model effectively fails to detect any instances of Heartbleed, highlighting the severe impact of extreme class imbalance on the detection of critically rare events. It is noteworthy that Web Attack - Sql Injection, despite having only 4 instances, was perfectly classified, suggesting that the patterns for this specific attack, though rare, might be more distinct or less ambiguous for the model to learn compared to Infiltration or Heartbleed.

These findings reinforce the observations of our confusion matrices (Fig. 1) and underscore that while our T5-based approach achieves the state of the art general accuracy, its effectiveness on extremely rare attack types is limited by the scarcity of training data for these specific categories. Future research will need to explore advanced techniques, such as data augmentation or synthetic data generation, to improve the detection capabilities of these minority classes.

5.4 Comparative Analysis with Related Work

To contextualize the performance of our proposed T5-based cyberattack detection system, we compare with state-of-the-art approaches (Section 2.2) applied to the CIC-IDS-2017 dataset.

Table 5. Comparative performance with state-of-the-art methods on CIC-IDS-2017

Method	Accuracy (%)	Precision (%)	Recall (%)	F-score (%)
Abdel-Basset et al. [1]	99.69	92.31	96.29	94.18
Wang et al. [24]	98.00	98.50	95.00	96.50
Maruthupandi et al. [9]	99.70	99.72	99.70	99.71
Guo et al. [5]	99.88	99.86	99.88	99.89
Hariharan et al. [7]	99.00	97.00	96.00	97.00
Tapu et al. [16]	95.68	96.50	95.68	96.10
Li et al. [8]	N/A	99.73	99.96	99.84
Yilmaz et al. [25]	N/A	93.00	71.00	74.00
Our work (Exp. 3)	**99.96**	**99.96**	**99.96**	**99.96**

As demonstrated in Table 5, our fine-tuned T5-based model (Experiment 3) outperforms or matches the reported accuracy and other key metrics of most existing methods on the CIC-IDS-2017 dataset. Notably, our accuracy of 99.96% is among the highest, surpassing even highly competitive approaches like [1] or [9]. While [8] report an F-score of 99.84% and recall of 99.96%, our approach demonstrates equally high and consistent performance across all metrics, including accuracy.

The superior performance of our method can be attributed to the powerful architecture of the T5 model, which, even after fine-tuning from an NLP-specific pre-training, effectively learns complex patterns from network flow statistics. This highlights the novelty and effectiveness of leveraging large pre-trained language models for diverse cybersecurity tasks, moving beyond traditional ANN architectures designed from scratch for this domain. This approach not only achieves high accuracy but also potentially benefits from the generalizable knowledge embedded within the large pre-trained models.

6 Conclusions and Future Work

We designed several experiments in order to study the influence of different factors, such as the size of the base model, using t5-small and t5-base, applied to the selected dataset, CIC-IDS-2017, using or removing the timestamp feature. The described experiments are part of our line of research in order to build a robust complex system for the detection of cyberattacks. For each experiment, we applied the technique called fine-tuning, over the different snapshots of T5, to adapt these models to our specific task of detecting cyberattacks. The selected dataset is public and contains information about statistics of network flows, focusing on the most recent and common types of attacks.

We cleaned and prepared the selected dataset for our experiments. We used the Stratified 5-Fold Cross-Validation technique to divide the data into two parts: 80% for training and validation, and 20% for testing. The 80% for training was divided further into five folds. In each training round, one fold was used for validation (16% of the total data), while the remaining four folds were used for training (64% of the total data). This process was repeated five times.

After training our models using fine-tuning, we successfully created several models which can detect cyberattacks. These models, originally designed for a very different purpose, have shown very high accuracy, approaching 100%. However, there is still room for improvement, especially in detecting SQL Injection attacks. This is likely due to the limited amount of training data available for this specific type of attack. This limitation impacts the model's ability to learn distinctive patterns. This observation is consistent with common challenges in highly imbalanced cybersecurity datasets and points towards the critical need for strategies to enhance the detection of such infrequent, yet potentially high-impact, threats.

As a next step, we are considering several ways to improve this research.

We achieved very promising results using the CIC-IDS-2017 dataset, especially in experiment 3, with an accuracy of 99.96% in classifying statistics of network traffic as benign or one of 14 different types of malicious attacks. To rigorously assess the model's generalisation capabilities, we intend to apply our methodology to other datasets. Since the CSE-CIC-IDS2018 dataset is considered the other dataset that contains the most modern and up-to-date types of attacks, we would like to apply our methodology to the newer dataset.

We used the fine-tuning technique for our main experiments, and the results were promising. However, we would like to try using a different technique called transfer learning, which could help us to obtain even better results. We plan to explore both approaches to determine the best method for our specific task.

We have been working on a system to detect cyberattacks using the fine-tuning technique over a NLP model. Since there are many different approaches we could apply to address this problem, we are interested in exploring a more traditional approach by building a custom model specifically for cyberattacks detection. By comparing the performance of these two methods, we can gain valuable insight into the best approach for this task.

Given the promising results that we have achieved using the smallest two versions of the T5 model, we are interested in exploring the performance of larger versions.

Finally, given the challenges observed with very rare attack types (e.g., Heartbleed, Infiltration), we plan to explore advanced data handling techniques. This includes investigating data augmentation strategies or synthetic data generation methods to improve the models' ability to accurately detect under-represented attack categories.

Acknowledgements. This publication is part of the I+D+i grant PID2021-122215NB-C33 funded by MICIU/AEI/10.13039/501100011033 and by ERDF/EU.

References

1. Abdel-Basset, M., Hawash, H., Chakrabortty, R.K., Ryan, M.J.: Semi-supervised spatiotemporal deep learning for intrusions detection in IoT networks. IEEE Internet Things J. **8**, 12251–12265 (2021). https://doi.org/10.1109/JIOT.2021.3060878
2. Of the Aegean, U.: The awid2 dataset (2016). https://icsdweb.aegean.gr/awid/awid2
3. BCCC: Behaviour-centric cybersecurity center (BCCC): cybersecurity datasets (2025). https://www.yorku.ca/research/bccc/ucs-technical/cybersecurity-datasets-cds/
4. Of the Aegean, U.: The awid3 dataset (2021). https://icsdweb.aegean.gr/awid/awid3
5. Guo, D., Xie, Y.: Research on network intrusion detection model based on hybrid sampling and deep learning. Sensors **25**(5) (2025). https://doi.org/10.3390/s25051578
6. Gutiérrez-Galeano, L., Domínguez-Jiménez, J.J., Schäfer, J., Medina-Bulo, I.: Llm-based cyberattack detection using network flow statistics. Appl. Sci. **15**(12) (2025). https://doi.org/10.3390/app15126529. https://www.mdpi.com/2076-3417/15/12/6529

7. Hariharan, S., Annie Jerusha, Y., Suganeshwari, G., Syed Ibrahim, S.P., Tupakula, U., Varadharajan, V.: A hybrid deep learning model for network intrusion detection system using seq2seq and convlstm-subnets. IEEE Access **13**, 30705–30721 (2025). https://doi.org/10.1109/ACCESS.2025.3541399
8. Li, Y., Qin, T., Huang, Y., Lan, J., Liang, Z., Geng, T.: HDFEF: a hierarchical and dynamic feature extraction framework for intrusion detection systems. Comput. Secur. **121**, 102842 (2022). https://doi.org/10.1016/j.cose.2022.102842
9. Maruthupandi, J., Sivakumar, S., Dhevi, B.L., Prasanna, S., Priya, R.K., Selvarajan, S.: An intelligent attention based deep convoluted learning (IADCL) model for smart healthcare security. Sci. Rep. **15**(1), 1363 (2025)
10. Raffel, C., Shazeer, N., Roberts, A., Lee, K., Narang, S., Matena, M., Zhou, Y., Li, W., Liu, P.J.: Exploring the limits of transfer learning with a unified text-to-text transformer. CoRR **1910**, 10683 (2020)
11. Roy, S.: Simplet5 (2022). https://github.com/Shivanandroy/simpleT5
12. Shafi, M., Lashkari, A.H., Roudsari, A.H.: Ntlflowlyzer: towards generating an intrusion detection dataset and intruders behavior profiling through network and transport layers traffic analysis and pattern extraction. Comput. Secur. **148**, 104160 (2025). https://doi.org/10.1016/j.cose.2024.104160. https://www.sciencedirect.com/science/article/pii/S0167404824004656
13. Sharafaldin, I., Habibi Lashkari, A., Ghorbani, A.A.: Toward generating a new intrusion detection dataset and intrusion traffic characterization. In: Proceedings of the 4th International Conference on Information Systems Security and Privacy - ICISSP, pp. 108–116. INSTICC, SciTePress (2018). https://doi.org/10.5220/0006639801080116
14. Sharafaldin, I., Lashkari, A.H., Hakak, S., Ghorbani, A.A.: Developing realistic distributed denial of service (DDOS) attack dataset and taxonomy. In: 2019 International Carnahan Conference on Security Technology (ICCST), pp. 1–8 (2019). https://doi.org/10.1109/CCST.2019.8888419
15. Sokolova, M., Lapalme, G.: A systematic analysis of performance measures for classification tasks. Inf. Process. Manag. **45**, 427–437 (7 2009). https://doi.org/10.1016/j.ipm.2009.03.002
16. Tapu, S., Shopnil, S., Tamanna, R., Dewan, M., Alam, M.: Malicious data classification in packet data network through hybrid meta deep learning. IEEE Access **11**, 140609–140625 (2023). https://doi.org/10.1109/ACCESS.2023.3341911
17. UNB: NSL-KDD dataset (2009). https://www.unb.ca/cic/datasets/nsl.html
18. UNB: CICFlowMeter (2016). https://www.unb.ca/cic/research/applications.html#CICFlowMeter
19. UNB: Intrusion detection evaluation dataset (CIC-IDS2017) (2017). https://www.unb.ca/cic/datasets/ids-2017.html
20. UNB: DDOS evaluation dataset (CIC-DDOS2019) (2019). https://www.unb.ca/cic/datasets/ddos-2019.html
21. UNB: IPS/IDS dataset on AWS (CSE-CIC-IDS2018) (2018). https://www.unb.ca/cic/datasets/ids-2018.html
22. UNSW: KDD cup 1999 data (1999). http://kdd.ics.uci.edu/databases/kddcup99/kddcup99.html
23. UNSW: The UNSW-NB15 dataset (2015). https://research.unsw.edu.au/projects/unsw-nb15-dataset

24. Wang, J., Wang, X.: An optimization model of computer network security based on GABP neural network algorithm. EURASIP J. Inf. Secur. **2025**(1), 1–17 (2025)
25. Yilmaz, M., Bardak, B.: An explainable anomaly detection benchmark of gradient boosting algorithms for network intrusion detection systems. In: Proceedings - 2022 Innovations in Intelligent Systems and Applications Conference, ASYU 2022 (2022). https://doi.org/10.1109/ASYU56188.2022.9925451

Author Index

J. Schäfer and J. Boubeta-Puig (Eds.): SGSOACS 2025, CCIS 2831, p. 149, 2026.
https://doi.org/10.1007/978-3-032-14816-2

The manufacturer's authorised representative in the EU is Springer Nature Customer Service Centre GmbH, Europaplatz 3, 69115 Heidelberg, Germany. If you have any concerns regarding our products, please contact ProductSafety@springernature.com

Printed and bound by CPI Group (UK) Ltd, Croydon, CR0 4YY
07/07/2026
02160929-0001